Russell Grant's
Astro-Tarot

Card Illustrations by Kay Smith

Dedicated to my mum, Joan,
without whose encouragement and love
the cards would never have been spread

Virgin

First published in Great Britain in 1992 by
Virgin Books
an imprint of Virgin Publishing Ltd
332 Ladbroke Grove
London W10 5AH

Reprinted with revisions 1993

A catalogue record for this book is available from the British Library

ISBN 0 86369 610 4

Development and Editorial Direction: Lewis Esson Publishing
Art Direction: Adrian Morris
Text Editor: Jane Struthers
Editorial Assistant: Jennifer Jones

Production by Imago Publishing, Thame, Oxfordshire
Typeset by Avocet Typesetters, Bicester, Oxfordshire
Colour separations by Bright Arts, Hong Kong
Printed and packaged for Imago in Hong Kong

Contents

WELCOME TO THE FASCINATING WORLD of the tarot! If you are new to this ancient art of divination, I trust that this book and my unique Astro-Tarot pack will awaken your interest in it, and if you are already familiar with the tarot, then I hope my pack of completely new cards will open up fresh avenues and inspirations for you to explore!

Most people know me first and foremost as an astrologer, but in fact I worked with tarot cards long before I started studying the stars. I've always found the tarot uncannily accurate, because it seems unerringly to pinpoint problems or predicaments, or herald good times that are just around the corner. Incidentally, many people think the tarot is all doom and gloom. They imagine every reading is going to be full of bad news and dire warnings, and take fright at the sight of any card that looks vaguely menacing or unfortunate, such as the cards named Death or the Tower (which really mean regeneration and change). Well, let me assure you once and for all that, like life, the tarot pack is a mixture of happiness and sadness, good and bad, optimism and pessimism.

THE CLASSIC TAROT

The origins of tarot cards are far from clear, but it is thought the first known tarot pack was created in Italy in the fourteenth century – although the tarot may have originally been devised either by Indian gypsies or the Celts. What is certainly true is that the tarot has borrowed ideas and images from all sorts of cultures, religions and ancient myths, and also from astrology, to create the images that appear on the cards. They are rich in symbolism and can give you glimpses into your own subconscious and behaviour (or that of the people around you) as well as providing an insight into the future.

The classic tarot pack is large, with 78 cards, and is divided into two main sections – the Major and Minor Arcana. The 22 cards of the Major Arcana are picture cards (also known as trump cards) and are full of symbolism. The 56 'pip' cards of the Minor Arcana are like ordinary playing cards, and are divided into 4 suits of 14 cards each (comprising 4 court cards and 10 'pip' cards numbered from the Ace to 10).

The cards in the Major Arcana represent all the phases of life we experience, from the innocence and naivety of the first card, the Fool, through to the sense of completion and fulfilment of the final card, the World. The cards of the Minor Arcana are divided into four suits – Cups, Pentacles (sometimes called Coins), Wands (sometimes called Rods or Staves) and Swords – to symbolize the four main aspects of life. These Minor Arcana cards are the ones that gave birth to the ordinary packs of playing cards we know today, but the suits were given different names – Cups became hearts, Pentacles were called diamonds, Wands were called clubs and Swords became spades.

The medieval Italians used to play a game called Tarocchi with their tarot cards, using the pip cards in the same way as we do today in card games and having the Major Arcana as trump cards. However, I wouldn't recommend using your tarot deck for card games because that is not what it is meant for and you will upset the vibrations of the cards if you don't treat them with respect.

Interpreting the cards

In some tarot packs only the Major Arcana cards are given symbolic pictures, with the Minor Arcana cards just showing the number of their particular suit, while other packs illustrate every single card. However, no matter how many cards are illustrated, their pictures aren't meant to be taken literally (and that applies to my Astro-Tarot pack, too) – for example, if you turn up the Magician card, it doesn't mean you are going to meet a conjuror or member of the Magic Circle! Instead, the image on the card is a symbol that must be interpreted, so the Magician means you should make the most of your abilities and dazzle others with your innate brilliance. However, don't worry, because in this book I give a detailed interpretation of each card in my Astro-Tarot pack, plus a brief description of its symbolism to give you a broader understanding of the underlying meanings of the tarot.

MY ASTRO-TAROT PACK

By now I expect you're wondering what is so different about my Astro-Tarot pack. Well, I had been using the classic tarot pack for years when I first began to think about devising my own version instead, about 15 years ago. Many people are familiar with the ordinary pack, but I wanted to create something new, exciting and innovative, combining my knowledge of the tarot with my experience of astrology.

I wanted to keep the 22 Major Arcana cards of the classic tarot because they are so important and rich in meaning, mythology and wisdom, but because the Minor Arcana deals with the nitty gritty details of life I felt it would be a challenge to create my own interpretation of them, drawing on my knowledge of astrology. Incidentally, that doesn't mean the cards of the traditional Minor Arcana are unimportant or out-of-date, simply that I wanted to devise my own version of them, using fresh and different images. So what exactly does my Astro-Tarot pack consist of?

Taking them in their numerical order (which is the order followed in this book), these are the cards I chose.

☐ First come **the 22 cards of the Major Arcana**, which are so steeped in symbolism. Because the Fool, which is the first card of the Major Arcana, traditionally doesn't have a number these cards are numbered from 0–21.

☐ Next come **the aces of the 4 suits from the traditional Minor Arcana** (Pentacles, Wands, Swords and Cups). I kept the aces because they represent new beginnings and assertion (or a lack of it). They are numbered from 22–25.

☐ After them are **the 12 Sun signs of the Western zodiac**, which run from Aries to Pisces. I chose them because they represent the cosmic journey we take through life. They are numbered from 26–37.

☐ **The 12 signs of the Chinese horoscope** follow next, running from the Rat to the Boar. I included them because Chinese horoscopes are based on the movements of the Moon, and therefore represent our emotions, senses, psychic side and spirituality. They are numbered from 38–49.

☐Last, but by no means least, come the final **14 cards which are all associated with Western astrology**. Interspersed with cards for each of the 9 planets in our Solar System (to represent our energy force, the influences around us and the people we will meet), are 5 cards of other astrological significance – the New and Full Moons (which represent man's life from birth to death), the Ascendant (which pinpoints our personality), the Midheaven (which guides our aspirations) and the Moon's Node (which concerns our karma, the lessons we must learn through life and the universal law that as you sow, so shall you reap). They are numbered from 50–63.

Take a look at the list of cards at the front of the book and at our handy guide on the cover of the book to familiarize yourself with the cards in the pack. Don't panic – as the cards start numbering in the traditional way from 0, the last card in the pack is number 63 – so there <u>are</u> 64 cards altogether. In numerology 6 and 4 add up to 1 ($6 + 4 = 10$, $1 + 0 = 1$), which is the divine number!

The design of the cards

At this stage, it's a good idea to spread the cards out in front of you and have a close look at them, because the sooner you become familiar with them the better. Start by looking at the cards of the Major Arcana – you'll see they're very different from traditional tarot cards because their pictures are lighter, brighter and really accentuate the positive in life without trivializing or ignoring the negative.

For instance, the traditional illustration for the Death card (number 13 in the pack) shows a skeleton (sometimes called the reaper) using a scythe on some ground that is littered with skulls. Although the card means transformation and rebirth in a mental, emotional or spiritual way, seeing a picture like that instantly makes you think of physical death and sends shivers down your spine – an image of the tarot I wanted to get away from. That's why the illustration for the Death card in my Astro-Tarot pack shows a skull (to symbolize an ending) with a beautiful red rose growing out of it (to show new life arising from that ending).

I devised the cards with a brilliant illustrator called Kay Smith. We spent many hours together discussing the essence and symbolism of the tarot and astrology to create illustrations that are unique to my Astro-Tarot pack, and I think she's designed a wonderful pack of cards. As you look through the deck yourself you'll see that I've chosen characters from fairy tales to represent most of the Sun signs, people portraying the animals they represent for the Chinese signs, and images of the ancient Roman gods for the planets. Not only are all the cards attractive, friendly and inviting, but they've been specially designed to give you plenty of clues about their meanings when you come to give your readings. These clues are also described with the meanings for each of the cards.

Now you know a little about the history of the classic tarot and of my unique Astro-Tarot pack, you can begin to get to know the cards themselves. The more you handle them and read their interpretations in this book, the more familiar you'll become with them and the better readings you'll give. Take things slowly, be patient and you'll discover a fascinating new technique that will never fail to inform and amaze you. Good luck!

IF YOU'VE NEVER USED A PACK of tarot cards before then you'll be delighted to discover how simple they are, and can look forward to many fascinating hours spent reading the cards for yourself, your family and friends. First, however, there are just a few simple rules to follow to ensure you get the best use out of these unique Astro-Tarot cards which I have designed especially for you.

Looking after the deck

If you haven't already done so, unwrap the deck of cards, spread them out and have a good look at them. Examine the different images, not only for the traditional Major Arcana but also the other cards. You may want to pay special attention to the cards representing your Sun sign and Chinese sign, and those of your nearest and dearest. Well, carry on, because the more familiar you are with the cards, the better your Astro-Tarot readings will be!

You must thoroughly mix up the cards before you can use them to give readings because otherwise, just like ordinary playing cards, they won't work properly or give you an accurate reading. A good way to do this is to place them all face down on a large table and then swirl them around with your hands until they get thoroughly mixed up. You might like to do this several times until you're sure the cards are as jumbled up as possible, then gather them all together again (but make sure they are all still face down). By this time some of the cards are bound to have got turned upside down in relation to one another but don't worry about that because this is also important for deeper interpretations, as you'll see in a minute. Whatever you do, don't be tempted to put the deck back in its original order whenever you finish using it, because you'll only have to jumble it up again next time you use it!

It is important that you keep your Astro-Tarot deck in a safe place and don't let anyone else touch it, except when you are giving readings, otherwise the cards can become contaminated with other people's vibrations and they won't work properly. If that happens, you can recharge the deck by sleeping with it under your pillow (or trying to – it's very lumpy!) Ideally, when not in use the deck should be wrapped in a piece of silk, such as a scarf, and kept in a wooden box (or anything else made from natural materials), to insulate it from other people's vibrations, but just wrapping the cards in a silk scarf should do just as well.

The meanings of the cards

The more familiar you are with the meanings of the Astro-Tarot cards the better and more fluent your readings will be, so spend lots of time reading what the cards mean and looking at the cards themselves. Even so, there's no need to learn their meanings by heart! The picture on each card will tell you a lot about that card's symbolism, and its interpretation in this book will be full of little clues that'll help you remember the meaning of the card.

As you look at the cards you'll see each picture has a right way up and a wrong way up, both of which will affect their meaning. For example, on most cards there is a seated or standing figure, or a face, so it is obvious which is the right way up. Where it is not immediately obvious the text in the book relating to each card will tell you. When a card appears the right way up, you should read the divinatory meaning for it on the relevant page of this book, and when it appears the wrong way up (upside down), you should read its reversed meaning. This reversed meaning is often the opposite of the card's meaning when it is the right way up. However, if you've never used the tarot before you might prefer to begin by using all the cards the right way up to give simpler readings. You can either do this by ensuring all the cards are turned the right way up before you deal them out or turning any reversed cards in a spread round the right way at the start of each reading.

*Upright
(Divinatory
meaning)* *Reversed
(Reversed
meaning)*

You can do readings with upright and reversed cards later on when you feel more confident.

Reading the upright and reversed meanings whilst looking at the relevant card will increase your understanding and help you to memorize its significance that much quicker (if that's what you want to do). After that, the more you use the cards and refer to this book, the better you'll become at interpreting my Astro-Tarot pack.

Once your family and friends know you're learning to read these cards you'll probably be deluged with requests to give them readings, but it's also a good idea to practise by yourself. After a few readings, instead of automatically looking up each card in this book try to remember its meaning by studying the illustration first, then check to see if you got it right. You'll be surprised at how quickly you begin to learn what the cards mean.

Shuffling the cards

Unlike an ordinary deck of playing cards, the way you shuffle and cut the cards is very important in Astro-Tarot. If you're giving a reading, you and the querent (the person who is being given the reading) should sit facing each other across a table, then you should shuffle the cards well. Now hand the deck to the querent and ask him or her to shuffle it too – they may shuffle it for as long as they like – and then cut it once with the hand he or she uses the least. He or she should then put what was the bottom pile of cards on what was the top pile of cards. Then ask the querent to select the number of cards required for the chosen spread from anywhere in the pack. (Obviously they must do this without turning the cards over to see what they are.) As they select them, they should make a pile of the selected cards, arranged face down just as they come from the pack. Again, they must be given as much time as they need for this process – don't hurry them! Once this pile is complete they should hand it to you directly across the table, without turning it round in any way – this is important as, if they accidentally turn them round, all the meanings may be reversed. The cards are now ready for your reading.

Incidentally, if you or the querent should drop a card at any stage of the reading, look up its basic meaning according to whether it is upright or reversed, because it's trying to get out of the pack and make its message known! For instance, if the querent were to drop the Star card while he or she was shuffling the cards and it fell upright, you would be able to announce the good news that the future is looking very rosy indeed for him or her, that a wish may be about to come true or a health problem will soon clear up.

Laying out the spread

To give a reading, the cards are arranged in special patterns called spreads. I have described four of them in detail on pages 10–15, with examples, so you can see exactly how they work. Ask the querent to choose which spread he or she wants, but try not to get carried away and start off with one of the more complicated spreads that use twelve cards! It's best to start with either the Horseshoe or Gypsy spreads (with seven or three cards respectively) and then progress to the longer ones when you're more confident!

Lay out the cards face down in the pattern of your chosen spread, dealing them off the top of the pile of cards that you have just taken from the querent. Turn the cards over away from you. It is likely that some of the cards may be upside down – if you are ignoring the reversed meanings of the cards at this stage you should turn these round.

Interpreting the spread

Before you begin referring to their interpretations, take time to examine the cards for any particular patterns because they can tell you a lot about the general feel of a spread. For example, a lot of Major Arcana cards suggest the querent is going through important changes or circumstances beyond his or her control, whilst a majority of Sun sign cards could suggest that the querent should alter or adapt his or her attitude to life in the manner of the particular cards. Many reversed cards could indicate delays, worries, setbacks and problems in general. If you do several spreads for one querent you may find that some cards appear again and again. If so, you should pay particular attention to their meanings as they are obviously very important cards for the querent at the time of the reading.

Now you are ready to interpret each card in turn with the help of this book. Sometimes you will find cards that seem to contradict the other ones in the spread, and that's when you should make the most of your intuition. If the meaning in this book seems odd then try to think of an alternative that fits in with the general definition of the card but also applies to the querent. It's best to practise on close family and friends at first, but remember the more you use the cards, the better and more adept you'll become at interpreting them.

It is also very important when reading the cards to give out what you feel intuitively. Use the cards as prompts to trigger your innate psychic powers and don't resist them. For instance, should the name of a person or place – or even a sense of joy or foreboding – pop into your head when you look at a card then include it in your reading, it may be relevant.

No one knows why, but the timing of the tarot can sometimes be rather strange and not as accurate as you might expect. Although some of the spreads described in this book are used to predict events during a specific time, such as the year, week or day ahead, the events foretold do not always take place within the chosen period. That is why it's always a good idea to write down the date of your reading and a note of each card with a brief interpretation of it, so you can check up later on.

Cards are reversed when viewed from the reader's perspective and not from the querent's position – unless you're giving yourself a reading, and then it's obvious!

A word of warning!

Be very careful when reading the cards for other people, especially at first. Even if they're jokey and glib on the surface, they will probably take your reading very seriously indeed inside so it's important not to alarm or upset them. Lots of people are wary or even frightened of the tarot because of its powerful images and reputation for being so uncannily accurate, so it's up to you to reassure your querents when you give them readings. If such cards as Death or the Hanged Man appear in a spread, you must explain that they can be very positive cards and don't mean your querent will drop dead or be executed before the end of the week! Instead, for the Death card you should say it signifies transformation and regeneration, and that the Hanged Man means the querent is in limbo between one situation and another, or may soon make sacrifices that will actually improve his or her life.

Even if you have to interpret a spread that seems negative, gloomy or depressing in the extreme and with little hope for the future, you mustn't say so to your querent. Although it is your duty to inform them – as forewarned is fore-armed – try to tone it all down as much as you can, even if he or she does tell you at a later date that things were much worse than you predicted. Better that than send your querent off shaking with fear!

THE DIFFERENT SPREADS

There are all sorts of different tarot spreads you can use, but I have chosen four for this book – the Horoscope, Horseshoe, Gypsy spreads and the Quickie. Once you are familiar with them you can use these Astro-Tarot cards in conjunction with the spreads given in other tarot books if you wish, or even make up your own!

The Horoscope spread

This is the largest of the spreads in this book, as it uses twelve cards. It can be interpreted in two ways: you can either use it to gain a detailed picture of the querent's life at the time of the reading or you can use it to predict the coming year of the querent, using a card a month. The cards are laid down and read in the same way for both interpretations.

A reading for the querent's life

The first interpretation of this spread, which describes in detail the querent's life at the time of the reading, involves the astrological idea of life being divided into twelve segments or astrological houses, each of which has a particular meaning. Throughout the book you'll find a brief interpretation of what each card means when it's in each of these twelve astrological houses, but the more you use and understand the cards, the more you'll be able to expand on these interpretations. Remember, listen to your intuition when reading the cards, for that's what makes a good accurate and enlightened tarot reader!

Here is a checklist describing the area of life governed by each astrological house, to help you still further in your interpretations.

The First House The querent himself or herself; his or her image, appearance and personality; personal projects and plans, health and well-being.

The Second House Money; possessions; spiritual and material values; major purchases and investments; whatever matters most to the querent in an earthly sense.

The Third House Communications (letters, calls, discussions etc); short trips; modes of travel; the everyday world; mental interests; the community; neighbours; learning; siblings.

The Fourth House The home and anything associated with it; relatives; family ties; security; the past; memories; women, but especially the querent's mother; emotions.

The Fifth House Love affairs, leisure and pleasure; the heart's desires; creativity and self-expression; sports and athletics; babies and children; pets; enjoyment; entertainment; holidays; celebrations; enterprises based on your own talents.

The Sixth House Work; service and business; subordinates; health and medical matters.

The Seventh House Partnerships of all kinds; marriage; relationships; open adversaries.

The Eighth House Shared money matters; sex and intimate affairs; intense emotions; income tax and other official dealings; regeneration and transformation; life/death issues.

The Ninth House Travel; other countries and cultures; religions and beliefs; philosophy; knowledge; higher or further education; the law; ecological affairs; a wider vision of the world.

The Tenth House Prestige; status; honour; career; direction in life; ambitions; achievements; father figures; success.

The Eleventh House Long-term plans; hopes and wishes; friendships; societies; clubs; group activities; hobbies; humanitarian ideals; the future.

The Twelfth House Seclusion; self-sacrifice; spirituality; the subconscious; dreams and reveries; institutions (hospitals, prisons etc); escapism; psychic powers; secrets; hidden fears, phobias and enemies; romance.

Here is an example of a reading that describes the current state of a querent's life:

FIRST HOUSE – EMPRESS CARD (No 3) The Empress card (see page 22) represents friendly women and a happy atmosphere, while the first house represents all personal matters. When the Empress is in the first house it is telling the querent to stay on an even keel, keep cool, calm and collected and then things will go his or her way. The friendly nature of the Empress means people are happy to help now.

The cards for this spread shoud be laid out and read in the order shown for both types of reading. This also indicates the positions of the houses.

See how easy it is . . .

SECOND HOUSE – OX CARD (No 39) REVERSED The reversed Ox card (see page 94) represents dogmatic behaviour, stubbornness, greediness and

a firm belief in oneself no matter what the situation, while the second house signifies money matters, investments and personal values. When the reversed Ox is in the second house, it means the querent will want to make some investments but could be deaf to anyone's advice or be determined to feather his or her own nest by doing others down. THIRD HOUSE – NODE CARD (No 63) REVERSED The reversed Node card (see page 142) is a warning, telling the querent not to make material matters the be-all and end-all otherwise life will deliver some hard lessons. The third house represents everyday affairs, dealings with neighbours and communications in general. When the reversed Node card is in the third house, you should warn the querent that negotiations or dealings could fail because he or she is too interested in their financial overtones, or there could be a row about someone's greedy attitude towards money. This is an example of the reader having to give the querent a tactful warning about possible problems ahead.

Incidentally, as two out of these three cards are reversed, there may be delays before the events forecast by the cards happen. Now that you can see how it's done why don't you try making your own readings based on the remaining cards in this spread: FOURTH HOUSE – CAPRICORN (No 35); FIFTH HOUSE – ACE OF SWORDS (No 24) REVERSED; SIXTH HOUSE – SATURN (No 57); SEVENTH HOUSE – ACE OF WANDS (No 23); EIGHTH HOUSE – LIBRA (No 32) REVERSED; NINTH HOUSE – MERCURY (No 50); TENTH HOUSE – JUDGEMENT (No 20); ELEVENTH HOUSE – VENUS (No 51); TWELFTH HOUSE – HORSE (No 44).

A reading for the year ahead

If you are using this spread for a month-by-month reading let the first card represent the current month, unless that month is nearly at an end (use your common sense for this, but as a rough guide I'd say the month is almost over on any date after the 20th), in which case it should represent the following one. The next card will represent the following month, and so on. Interpret each card using its relevant general divinatory or reversed meaning.

Here is an example of a reading for the year ahead. It was done in early April, so I took April as the first month.

APRIL – MOON CARD (No 18) The interpretation for the Moon card (see page 52) talks of highly-charged emotions and possible deceit. So, for this month, the querent should take care as feelings will be running high, and someone may even try to pull the wool over their eyes or create a mystery. The Moon is generally regarded as a feminine influence, so the card also means that a woman could cause trouble.

MAY – ACE OF CUPS CARD (No 25) The Ace of Cups (see page 66) means the start of a new relationship or fulfilment in a current one which could be anything from a deeply emotional love affair, a firm friendship or a strong working partnership. (The current circumstances of the querent or the other cards in the spread may make it obvious which sort of relationship it will be.) Because one of the card's traditional meanings is of a marriage in which a ring is given, it can also mean a lovely gift is on the way for the querent.

JUNE – RAT CARD (No 38) REVERSED When reversed, the Rat (see page 92) means con men, people who can sweet talk their way into anything or folk who are able to use their gift of the gab to get what they want. These traits may apply to the querent (in which case you should be tactful!), or to someone he or she is going to meet. Either way, this card is delivering a gentle warning about someone's behaviour, so pass it on to your querent. And so on . . . Again, why don't you practise on the remaining cards in this spread: JULY – ASCENDANT (No 61); AUGUST – GEMINI (No 28); SEPTEMBER – JUPITER (No 56); OCTOBER

– ARIES (No 26) REVERSED; NOVEMBER – DRAGON (No 42) REVERSED; DECEMBER – DEVIL (No 15); JANUARY – PISCES (No 37); FEBRUARY – MERCURY (No 50); MARCH – URANUS (No 58).

The Horseshoe spread

This spread uses seven cards to show the trends for the coming week. You read one card for each day, before making a general summing up of the week ahead. If you're reading this spread in the evening, make the first card represent the following day. Read the cards from their general divinatory or reversed interpretations.

Here is an example:

Day 4

Day 3   *Day 5*

Day 2   *Lay the cards out and read*   *Day 6*

Day 1   *them in the numerical order shown*   *Day 7*

DAY 1 – CHARIOT CARD (No 7) The Chariot card (see page 30) represents drive, assertiveness and energy, and promises success if you have faith in yourself. It could be interpreted as saying the first day will be a good one for plenty of hard work but the rewards will be rich, so the querent should do his or her best and not lose heart. The Chariot is a form of transport, so this would be a good time to buy or sell a car.

DAY 2 – HIEROPHANT CARD (No 5) REVERSED The Hierophant card when reversed (see page 26) means the querent should be unconventional or more spiritual. It also means someone may annoy or irritate him or her. You could interpret the card by telling the querent that being unconventional will win the day or that he or she should come off the material plane. There may be difficulty in understanding someone's belief or faith: a relationship or union may be irreconcilable.

DAY 3 – EARTH CARD (No 52) The Earth card (see page 120) is linked with nature, the environment and conservationism, and also practical and down-to-earth behaviour. You could therefore interpret that it means the querent will be feeling practical and matter-of-fact. The card's association with nature suggests it will be a good day for doing some gardening or getting involved in an environmental matter. Global issues predominate.

And so on . . . Again, as you can see how easy it is, you finish the reading by interpreting the remaining cards:

DAY 4 – SNAKE (No 43); DAY 5 – FOOL (No 0); DAY 6 – MONKEY (No 46); DAY 7 – NEPTUNE (No 59).

The Gypsy spread

Like the Horoscope spread, this has two interpretations. One uses three cards to show the trends for a given day – the first card represents the morning, the second the afternoon and the third the evening. The second uses three cards to represent the past, present and

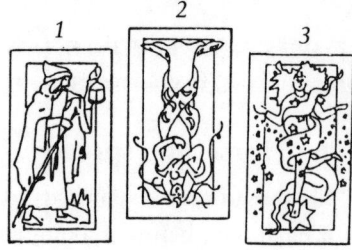

future. Read the cards from their general divinatory or reversed interpretations.

The spread for a particular day works like the Horseshoe spread, but uses less cards, of course. Here is an example of using the cards to represent the past, present and future:

PAST – HERMIT CARD (No 9) The Hermit card (see page 34) signifies withdrawal, the need to be alone and the ability to use one's mind to see the way forward. When it describes the querent's past, you could interpret it by saying the querent has wanted to be by him- or herself and keep away from others. He or she may have had important decisions to think through or had to weigh up the pros and cons of a particular problem. The querent hasn't been feeling sociable and has preferred his or her own company.

PRESENT – HIGH PRIESTESS CARD (No 2) REVERSED When reversed, the High Priestess card (see page 20) suggests the querent is ignoring his or her intuitions and feelings, and might therefore make the wrong decisions. The querent must tune into his or her inner self. To describe the querent's present, you could advise tuning into his or her intuitions, otherwise arguments or problems that could have been prevented might be stirred up. The querent must work out what he or she wants from life. A highly psychic and mystical time.

FUTURE – STAR CARD (No 17) The Star card (see page 50) symbolizes hope, optimism, unexpected blessings, long-awaited rewards and recognition. It also means feeling better after a long illness. When describing the future, you can tell the querent that it will be rosy and happy, and will go the way he or she wishes. Because the card represents happiness, loved ones and superiors will show their appreciation. If the querent has been waiting for someone to discover his or her true worth then this is when it will happen.

Incidentally, the fact that all three cards are from the Major Arcana means the reading is a very important and fateful one for the querent.

The Quickie

This is a good way of answering a particular question of the querent. First, the querent says aloud what his or her question is. Then, after cutting the deck in the usual way, the querent chooses a single card from the pack (without looking to see what it is, of course!) and hands it to the reader, who answers the querent's question according to the interpretation of the single card, taken from its general divinatory or reversed interpretation. You will be amazed at the accuracy of this simple method! Here is an example:

QUESTION – Should I take the new job that's been offered to me?

ANSWER – WORLD CARD (No 21) Yes! The World card (see page 58) means total fulfilment, spiritual enlightenment, the completion of a phase in life and appreciation by others. New opportunities are on the way. When interpreting the card as the answer to this question you can tell the querent that he or she has reached the end of a phase in life and is now ready to move on to fresh pastures and better things. This card says there are new adventures, and possibly lots of travel, on the way. The new job will offer all sorts of grand opportunities and bring the querent success.

DEVELOPING YOUR OWN SPREADS

When you become more confident with the Astro-Tarot and have had plenty of practise in interpreting the cards, you might like to start developing your own spreads. You could devise simple ones, perhaps with four cards to represent family, career, love and health, or anything other category that seems applicable at the time. The more you get to know the Astro-Tarot, the more you'll discover which spreads work best for you.

Another idea for a quick reading is based on the twelve houses of the horoscope (see page 10), in which you choose the number of cards that are assigned for your particular question. However, although there are twelve houses in the zodiac I've only used six, because otherwise what should be a quick reading will become very long and complicated indeed!

Shuffle and cut the cards in the usual way, then deal out the number of cards you require. The different categories are listed below under the number of cards to use. For example, if you wanted to know whether a party you're throwing is going to be a success, you would deal out five cards, or just choose one card for any personal question.

ONE CARD All personal matters; your appearance; new beginnings and men.

TWO CARDS Money matters; investments; financial worries; possessions; your self-esteem; your sex life; women.

THREE CARDS Everyday concerns; travel; neighbours and siblings; communications.

FOUR CARDS The home and family matters; the past; dealings with parents.

FIVE CARDS Love affairs; relationships; creativity; celebrations; holidays; leisure; the future.

SIX CARDS Your working world; health matters; worries; subordinates; secrets.

Now that you understand the basic principles of the way the tarot works and how it is used, we come to the heart of my Astro-Tarot – the meanings of each of the cards. As you know, every one of them has been devised by me to express the best of the tarot and astrology, based on the knowledge I have gained over many years of studying both subjects.

Throughout the rest of this book each card (which appears in the numerical order shown on the cards) is given two pages to itself to make the book as easy to use as possible. The first interpretation given for each card is the divinatory meaning, which is its essential meaning and the one you should use for the annual reading of the Horoscope spread, the Horseshoe, Gypsy and Quickie spreads. The next explanation tells you how to interpret the card if it appears reversed. Remember that a reversed card can mean delays or that the divinatory meaning of the card has been reversed (so what was fortunate becomes less so, or vice versa). After this come the interpretations of each card as it will appear in each of the twelve houses in the full astrological reading of the Horoscope spread.

It's bound to take you some time to become familiar with all the meanings of the cards, but don't be disappointed or downhearted if you have to go back over them time and time again. That is what this companion book to my Astro-Tarot pack is for – it is your guide to the mysteries of the tarot.

Now you are ready to take your first steps. Start looking through the cards again so you become familiar with what they look like and read through each one's meaning, then, when you're ready, practise with some of the simple spreads. Using my Astro-Tarot pack will soon become second nature, so don't worry. All you need do is turn the page . . .

0 Fool

Divinatory meaning

This is the most important card in the pack because it represents not just the individual but human nature - with its failings as well as its successes. When it appears in a spread it indicates a time of fresh beginnings, when you will step into the unknown.

A door is opening in your world, revealing anything from a new job, relationship or abode to a complete change of direction in the way you live your life. You'll have to face challenges but you should be able to take them in your stride. You might even reveal all sorts of skills and talents you never knew you had, and you're bound to enjoy yourself along the way.

There's no doubt this is a positive card, but even so you must look before you leap. The card shows a young man stepping out high, wide and handsome, but isn't he about to walk off the edge of a cliff? The little dog by his side represents his conscience, but will it prevent him making false moves or lead him headlong into trouble? His sack represents the knowledge and intuition he has gathered through his life, but will he use it sensibly? Watch your step and all will be well.

Reversed meaning

Fools rush in where angels fear to tread, and you're about to plunge into a new situation or circumstance without any thought for the consequences.

Maybe you're obsessed by a pastime or project that ends up costing you too much time or money, or perhaps you're swept off your feet by someone who seems the perfect paramour, but have turned a blind eye to all the problems and pitfalls that this partnership will bring?

The advice and admonishments of well-meaning folk will probably fall on deaf ears now, but if you won't listen to others then you must heed that voice of conscience inside you.

You must look before you leap now otherwise you'll really come a cropper!

. . . in the First House

Hold it! You're full of excitement and energy but don't know what to do with it. Take stock of your life and think hard before swinging into action. Why not work out exactly what you want to achieve, then channel your energies in the right direction?

. . . in the Second House

If you're planning some serious wheeling and dealing then make sure you've got the money first, and don't gamble with anything you can't afford to lose. Beware of being flash with your cash or assuming you've got the Midas touch!

. . . in the Third House

Your mind may be working overtime and you could be rushing from pillar to post, but is it doing any good? It's all too easy to be a jack of all trades and fritter your energy away now, so think things through first and take them one step at a time.

. . . in the Fourth House
Life may have dealt you some blows lately but taking them out on your kith and kin is hardly going to help. Spend some time mulling over how much your home and family mean to you, then start putting your fond feelings into affectionate action.

. . . in the Fifth House
If pride goeth before a fall then make sure your feet are on the ground, otherwise you could come a cropper. If you've been swanning along hoping for the best then you must do some soul-searching and decide what you really want from life.

. . . in the Sixth House
If you're currently on a quest for personal perfection then stop and ask yourself what's really wrong. Is it connected with your job or a health worry? Then calm down, seek expert advice if necessary and start making changes for the better.

. . . in the Seventh House
Relationships aren't all they're cracked up to be and it's time to work out why. Ask yourself some serious and searching questions about what you want from your one-to-one affairs, and what you're prepared to give in return. You'll learn a lot.

. . . in the Eighth House
Got to sort out your shared financial affairs or paperwork connected with the taxman, insurances, pensions or wills? Then stop procrastinating and get cracking instead. If you've been keeping a sexual affair to yourself it could come to light now.

. . . in the Ninth House
Come down to earth! You're walking around with your head in the clouds, indulging in all sorts of daydreams and delusions, but it's time to return to real life! Start using your common sense instead of your imagination and adopt a practical approach.

. . . in the Tenth House
If you're in a quandary over your career or have made some business blunders lately then this is when you must review and revise your aims and ambitions, then throw yourself back into the swing of things. After that, matters can only improve.

. . . in the Eleventh House
You may hate the thought of conforming and being the same as everyone else, but you're about to go too far in the opposite direction and really rock the boat! If that's already happened then view your friends realistically and let time heal any rifts.

. . . in the Twelfth House
Are you lost in a whirl of confusing emotions, easy prey for folk out to deceive you or dogged by doom and despondency? Then tune into your powerful intuition and do some quiet meditation or soul-searching, and you'll soon be back on course.

1 *Magician*

Divinatory meaning

Traditionally, the Magician is supposed to represent Prometheus, who stole the gift of fire from the gods of heaven and brought it back to earth. Just like the characteristics assigned to this card, Prometheus was quick-witted and strong-willed - these qualities are illustrated on the card by the Magician's juggling (his dexterity) and also by his sceptre (his will power).

You could be about to embark on a new enterprise or venture, and it's your actions and abilities that will influence its success or failure. In fact, whatever your current circumstances, this is your chance to bring out your innate talents and attributes to the full. It's no time to be one of the crowd or to try to fit in with everyone else! Instead, you must show folk just how original, independent and inspired you really are. Use your charm, charisma and personal magnetism to win people over to your side, bedazzle them with your brilliant brainwaves and reveal your true self in all its glory.

If you're about to embark on a new business venture or major project, then this card is giving you the green light. Whatever tasks or topics you tackle now, you'll see them through from start to finish.

Reversed meaning

Watch out, for illusion is in the air! Maybe someone's about to practise a little trickery on you or perform some sleight of hand that'll really get you fooled? Alternatively, you could be the one who's weaving a few spells for your own ends!

Although you must keep your wits about you now, that doesn't mean you should automatically ignore opportunities that come your way, for one might be a winner! Instead, make sure you explore the ins and outs of any enterprise before committing yourself, especially if other people have invited you to get involved with their schemes. Once you know exactly what you're doing, then you can forge full steam ahead with confidence and charisma!

. . . in the First House

You're blessed with tremendous potential for getting things done now, so make the most of this wonderful chance to steer matters in the direction you want through the sheer force of your personality. Just make sure you aren't too cocky or confident.

. . . in the Second House

Even if you aren't usually a financial wizard you've got the Midas touch now, and with dogged determination and skilful manoeuvring you could come up trumps. There's no doubt you're inspired, especially where money and property are concerned.

. . . in the Third House

You've really got the gift of the gab now, ensuring you'll get on well with everyone you meet, and you'll be dashing hither and thither too. It's a grand time for wheeling and dealing, but make sure your brilliant brainwaves aren't just a lot of hot air.

. . . in the Fourth House

Charismatic and strong-willed, you've plenty of understanding and know how to use it intelligently. Kith and kin mean a lot to you and you're able to tune into their deepest desires and wishes, enabling you to forge strong links with loved ones.

. . . in the Fifth House

You're eager to enjoy fun and games and have got the flair to make all social settings go with a bang. Why not throw a wee party where you're the host or hostess with the mostest? Revelling in the company of dear ones will thrill you now.

. . . in the Sixth House

If there's any painstaking work to be done then you're the one to do it, thanks to your diligent, methodical and precise approach. You'll also enjoy preening yourself or your abode to perfection, but don't expect everyone else to reach your standards!

. . . in the Seventh House

Subtle and charming, you'll get on well with partners of all persuasions now, and if you're single then your powers of attraction will ensure you don't stay solo for long. Harmony is your watchword, making all encounters successful and happy.

. . . in the Eighth House

Get moving on all official or joint financial affairs now whilst you're able to handle them with considerable care and attention, and might even manipulate matters to your advantage. Don't ignore amorous affairs, though, for you're a sexual star now!

. . . in the Ninth House

High-minded, spiritual or intellectual matters see you excel at the moment, for your mind's able to grasp all sorts of serious and contemplative concepts, and come up with some original ideas of your own to boot. Athletic activities are ace as well.

. . . in the Tenth House

You've certainly got the magic touch in business and career matters, and it's all thanks to your current determination and will to succeed. Promotion, prestige and pre-eminence are all within your grasp now, so cash in whilst you can!

. . . in the Eleventh House

Dare to be different! Now's the time to let your hair down, act unconventionally and forget about your usual code of conduct. Give your normal haunts a miss and try out an exciting new pub or club that'll introduce you to fresh faces and interests.

. . . in the Twelfth House

Are you carrying around needless guilts, regrets or excess emotional baggage from the past? Then it's time to banish them from your world by examining them in the cold light of day. Folk who've been agin you will come over to your side now.

2 High Priestess

Divinatory meaning

Tradition decrees that the High Priestess is the perfect woman and the embodiment of all that is feminine. She is believed to represent Isis, who was the ancient Egyptian goddess of fertility. On the card she not only looks like an Egyptian goddess but also holds a crystal ball to signify her wisdom and considerable psychic abilities.

A wise woman may be about to give you some helpful and valuable advice. Listen carefully to her, for she's full of integrity and can combine inspiration with sound common sense. She'll be especially helpful if you're wondering which way to turn or whether a new venture or enterprise is going to be a success, but don't just rely on her opinion.

This card has very strong psychic associations, and is telling you to tune into your own intuition to find the answers to your questions. Listen to that wee voice inside you and follow your gut feelings!

If you're about to embark on some serious study or further education then this is a grand card to pick, for it indicates your studies will go well and that you might also find a marvellous mentor or terrific teacher at the same time.

Reversed meaning

You seem to be ignoring your intuitions, feelings and needs, and that's going to make you very unhappy and out of step with yourself. As a result, you will make poor decisions, underestimate others as well as yourself and provoke arguments or antagonism galore. You must tune into the inner you, find out who you truly are (yes, warts and all!) and discover what you really want out of life. Only then will matters start to improve.

Perhaps part of the problem stems from having to place the needs and wishes of loved ones before your own? Try to leave them to their own devices as much as possible, for you also deserve some TLC, tender loving care.

Be honest with yourself, and you could learn a lot now.

. . . in the First House

You may have lots of get up and go, but can you channel it in the right direction? If you're not sure of the path you want to take then a teacher, mentor or intuitive woman could set you on the right track, but listen to your inner needs too.

. . . in the Second House

Even if you usually handle your cash concerns with care and confidence you'd do well to seek the advice of a money-minded maiden you meet now. Mull over her suggestions before making a move, but don't take risks if you can't afford them.

. . . in the Third House

The little brainwaves you're having could turn into blinding flashes of inspiration if you listen to them closely, but even so you may need help to steer them in the right direction. Maybe a woman of the world could open some mighty doors for you?

. . . in the Fourth House

Got problems with kith and kin? Then seek the sympathetic ear of a friendly female and stop bottling things up. She could give you just the advice and guidance you need to back up your innate intuition and understanding and pour oil on troubled waters.

. . . in the Fifth House

Dealings with dear ones aren't always easy now, for you sense you're out of tune with the VIPs of your heart. Even so, you're learning volumes about how to relate to others, and the inspired advice of a dear damsel will get you back on an even keel.

. . . in the Sixth House

The sound judgement of a chum or colleague will stand you in sterling stead where your health and work are concerned, so don't ignore or pooh-pooh the opinions of others. You could be told some terrific tips to make life go from strength to strength.

. . . in the Seventh House

There's always room for improvement in relationships, and a worldy-wise wench is about to give you some helpful hints about your one-to-one affairs. Partnerships of all persuasions will benefit now, so listen carefully to what she's got to say.

. . . in the Eighth House

Spoilt for choice when it comes to finding the right pension, insurance or long-term investment? Then pick the brains of a knowledgeable lady who's only too happy to help. An inheritance or tax problem might also need sorting out now.

. . . in the Ninth House

If you're thinking of spreading your wings and flying off to distant shores then lend an ear to the informed views and suggestions of a likeable lass. Whether you already know her or meet her on your trip, her opinions are well worth listening to.

. . . in the Tenth House

Prestigious and professional pursuits are going great guns now, but they'll be even better if you listen to a canny woman's words of wisdom. They could be just what you need to propel you further along the path to success, so pin back your ears!

. . . in the Eleventh House

You'd rather be unique than one of the crowd, and you're about to meet a maiden who's just as original as you. If you've been delving into the mystical and mysterious side of life then she could be just the person to guide you in the right direction.

. . . in the Twelfth House

Having strange or prophetic dreams? Then start writing them down before you jump out of bed. You could get chatting to an intuitive lady who can see straight into your subconscious. She may be a stranger, a friend or even your dear old mum!

3 Empress

Divinatory meaning

This lovely abundant, generous card has two distinct meanings.

Firstly, it symbolizes fertility (as shown by the plants growing up either side of the card – the Empress has been linked with Ceres, the Greek goddess of fertility), so could represent anything from a voluptuous young woman to a real earth-mother who makes you feel warm, safe and secure. It may mean there's a child on the way for the querent, or it can forecast news of a baby born to a relative or close chum. The Empress can also indicate a happy marriage (look at the hearts on her dress) or foretell that good times, with plenty of material comforts, will soon arrive.

On the other hand, this card can indicate a move to the countryside, or that gardening and growing your own food would be very satisfying and rewarding. Possessions will also be important and provide the security you need. If money's been scarce, then cash concerns may soon improve, or maybe you'll just feel happy with your lot. You'll also be doused in diplomacy and charm, making dealings with others pleasant and productive.

Reversed meaning

You could be feeling out of step with the world now, perhaps because of a lack of loot, emotional insecurity or trouble and strife at home. Beware of indulging in possessive or jealous behaviour, especially if you're frightened of losing a loved one, for that's the best way to do just that!

You might also feel frustrated with your current surroundings, particularly if you live in a town but want to be in the country, or long to make use of your green fingers.

A shortage of money may mean you have to tighten your boodle belt and economize on life's little luxuries.

If you're trying to have a baby, there could be reproductive or gynaecological problems now that lead to disappointment or disillusion which may or may not last.

. . . in the First House

All the vim and vitality bubbling away inside you will ensure folk fall over backwards to do your bidding, but you must stay on the right side of them and be sure of what you're doing. Keep on an even keel and don't give in to frustration or anger.

. . . in the Second House

There are rich pecuniary pickings to be made now if you play your cards right, but you must be sure of what you're doing. Speculating to accumulate could come up trumps given the right guidance, or leave you penniless if you put a foot wrong.

. . . in the Third House

Your mind's firing on all cylinders, ensuring ace communications and increasing your charm and charisma no end. Your way with words will win folk round to your mode of thinking but make sure you can deliver the goods before promising the earth!

. . . in the Fourth House

Kith and kin will delight in your loving, caring ways, and your current air of understanding and sympathy will make your abode a haven of happiness and security. Just don't go overboard and stifle your dear ones with smother love!

. . . in the Fifth House

You're oozing charm and a marvellous magnetic attraction at the moment, so no wonder all activities associated with love, leisure and pleasure are starred for success. Just don't become stubborn or too full of your own importance. Keep cool!

. . . in the Sixth House

What a hive of industry you are, keen to sort out petty problems and get everything organized. Well, that diligence will soon be rewarded by a pay rise or promotion, but don't lord it over your colleagues as a result. Remember, you're part of a team!

. . . in the Seventh House

Partnerships of all persuasions will benefit now from your friendly attitude, strong spirit of co-operation and deep need for harmony. Loving liaisons will be especially enjoyable, but don't forget you've got to give in order to receive.

. . . in the Eighth House

All your red-blooded passion could astound your amour at the moment, but don't spoil things by being too possessive or hot-headed. Shared money matters will see you acting like a soul inspired, and a wee windfall could be coming your way as well.

. . . in the Ninth House

Grab the chance to go travelling, whether for business or pleasure, and you'll have a whale of a time. Sporty pursuits will see you bursting with vitality too. A philosophical approach to life is grand but don't bite off more than you can chew.

. . . in the Tenth House

Golden opportunities are about to bless your career or prestige, and some inspired moves could earn you well-deserved promotion or clinch that lucrative deal. Just make sure you aren't in over your head and know exactly what you're doing.

. . . in the Eleventh House

Seek out unconventional people and places now and some terrific opportunities could follow. Not only will you have fun but you'll make some useful new connections too, although you must play fair and be prepared to give as much as you take.

. . . in the Twelfth House

Some honest soul-searching will be a real education now, teaching you volumes about your own motives, wishes and needs as well as revealing insights into what makes other folk tick too. Meditating quietly will show what's really needed in your life.

4 *Emperor*

Divinatory meaning

The male equivalent of The Empress, this authoritative card can represent a man who's endowed with worldly power, as shown by his crown, sceptre and orb. He could be someone in authority (symbolized by the throne) who enters your life now, such as a boss, bigwig or bureaucrat, he might be an older relative, such as a father, brother, uncle or grandfather, or perhaps a benificent and steadfast friend who can be counted on in times of trouble. He may also be a partner who's reliable and honest but won't ever set the world on fire! Even so, the scowl on the face of the Emperor shows he can give way to bouts of bad temper or impulsive behaviour at times.

Alternatively, this card can signify status and achievement, indicating that you are about to receive the rewards and recognition you deserve and will be able to climb up the ladder of success. Hard work will soon start to pay off, bringing you responsibilities, money and acclaim — you will be able to assume the Emperor's throne!

Reversed meaning

You may be dealing with a man who isn't quite what he seems. Perhaps he's putting on a big act and pretending to be stronger or more macho than he really is, he can't fulfill other people's expectations of him or he's hit a bad patch when he just can't cope with life?

On the other hand, you could come into contact with a fellow who's immature for his age, emotionally unrealistic or who lets you down at the last minute. He might also abandon projects and plans halfway through — or are you the one who's shirking your responsibilities, can't concentrate or is flitting from one task to another at the drop of a hat? If so, then work out what's wrong and decide how you can make things better for yourself.

. . . in the First House

You're exuding power and authority from every pore now and are certainly not in the mood for playing games or mucking about. Instead, make wise and controlled use of this strong-minded time whilst you get the chance, but don't turn into a dictator!

. . . in the Second House

It's a grand chance to boost your boodle bag, so handle all money matters in a controlled yet confident way that will show you really mean business. Even so, you should stash away some cash for a rainy day for your finances may not always be this good!

. . . in the Third House

You're the centre of attention now, with your finger in every pie. Your words of wisdom command respect from everyone who hears them, making it a marvellous opportunity to talk folk round to your way of thinking or come up trumps in commercial concerns.

. . . in the Fourth House

You're the tops as far as kith and kin are currently concerned, and what you say goes in your own abode. All the same, don't let this new-found power go to your head or make you imagine your word is law. Give the family a say in domestic decisions too!

. . . in the Fifth House

King pin! That's you at the moment, and you're revelling in being top dog both socially and romantically. What a wonderful excuse for going out on the town and enjoying the undivided attention of friends and loved ones! Enjoy it whilst it lasts!

. . . in the Sixth House

Workaday dealings see you shine now for you're the soul of efficiency, authority and organization. Colleagues, clients and employees will be dazzled by your superior skills and capacity for hard work and you'll be just as exacting in your own abode.

. . . in the Seventh House

You've got the upper hand in all one-to-one affairs now and are determined to make them as easy-going, harmonious and pleasant as possible. Your current spirit of co-operation will rub off on everyone around you, so make the most of it!

. . . in the Eighth House

Command and control are your watchwords now, making you a formidable force to be reckoned with and earning you the respect of everyone you meet. Use your brain and you'll handle any joint money matters with inspired insight and flawless flair.

. . . in the Ninth House

There's no need to adopt airs and graces for you've already won the admiration, attention and interest of the folk around you. If you're off on your travels then you'll take all eventualities in your stride. You're a star at the moment!

. . . in the Tenth House

At last, you're given the chance to prove your sterling worth in professional and prestigious pursuits. It's easy to take control or dish out the orders at the moment, and they'll be accepted with alacrity, but don't forget to mix might with mercy.

. . . in the Eleventh House

Even if you seem rather eccentric to others at least you've captured their interest and attention! In fact, whatever you do now others will follow, so why not lead your pals in some unconventional and different directions? Have fun!

. . . in the Twelfth House

You're so perceptive at the moment that folk will trust your judgement and intuition on almost anything, so make the most of your current ability to see straight to the heart of any matter. Just don't be surprised if everyone comes to you for advice!

5 Hierophant

Divinatory meaning

Also known as the Pope, the Hierophant symbolizes spirituality and a turning away from material matters towards more enlightened and high-minded affairs. The triple cross that he's holding represents the spiritual, intellectual and physical worlds, showing that a truly complete life combines all three of them.

This card often appears when you're dissatisfied with your life or have become bogged down in materialistic desires and cares. You may not know which way to turn, but the Hierophant's message is to look inside yourself for the answer and to adopt a more spiritual way of life. Reconciliation in a broken marriage is possible when this card appears.

When this card represents a person, it is usually a teacher, mentor or a professional expert, such as a doctor or lawyer, who can help you in some way. (The building in the background could be a cathedral or university.)

The Hierophant also represents a conventional or conservative outlook, telling you to stick to the true, tried and tested rather than branch out into unknown territory. Traditional actions and attitudes will be best now.

Reversed meaning

Unconventional methods will produce the desired results, and it's also a good idea not to force an issue but just to let things develop at their own pace. If you meet a new amour now then don't be disappointed if you both want very different things from the relationship.

You may also have to deal with someone who irritates or annoys you, but making excuses for their short-comings or letting them get away with murder won't do either of you any good. Instead, you should put your foot down and stand up for yourself. You must be cruel to be kind. There's no chance of a broken marriage being reconciled; it's over.

. . . in the First House

Whatever the worries besetting you now, deep down in your heart of hearts you know that you've got the answers. In fact, if you listen to that little voice inside you it'll not only tell you how to solve your own problems but also those of other people.

. . . in the Second House

Some folk say money makes the world go round, but you know that there's a lot more to life than just loot. Even though you've learned a lot lately about using your boodle to its best advantage, don't ignore all the things cash can't buy.

. . . in the Third House

Discussions, debates or even neighbourly natters could raise topics or reveal secrets that give you plenty of food for thought. They might even totally transform the way you look at life and give you an increased insight into spiritual subjects.

. . . in the Fourth House

Your current sensitivity and understanding, both of yourself and others, will delight kith and kin and ensure your abode is a place of happiness, harmony, affection and warmth. The more you lavish love on your dear ones the better life will be.

. . . in the Fifth House

The kindness and caring you're showing to loved ones now will ensure they clamour for your attention and adore your worldly-wise and magnetically attractive persona. All loving liaisons will benefit, and you might even meet the darling of your dreams!

. . . in the Sixth House

You're so keen, kind and considerate at work that folk will be thrilled by your co-operative spirit and pleasant attitude. Your health will benefit if you take a more philosophical approach to life or develop your innate spiritual leanings.

. . . in the Seventh House

The music of the spheres is resounding through your whole spirit, making you the model of kindness in one-to-one affairs and ensuring you're popular in business and pleasure alike. Combine that with a hint of authority and it's roses all the way!

. . . in the Eighth House

Perceptive isn't the word for you! You've got such insight that it makes folk tremble – you seem to know their every thought. You're potently passionate too, but intimate affairs will fare even better if you approach life from a spiritual slant.

. . . in the Ninth House

Even if you aren't remotely religious there's something other-worldly about your thinking now. Learning about what makes you tick will increase your understanding of the world around you, so investigate mystical or metaphysical matters.

. . . in the Tenth House

Understanding others is the key to career success now, whether you're at the top of your tree or a little fish in a big pond. Being honest with people, telling the truth and having the confidence to reveal the real you will also work wonders.

. . . in the Eleventh House

The lessons you learn now and the insights you have will stand you in super stead for the future, and also ensure your friendships go from strength to strength. Listen to your instincts, for they're transforming the way you see the world.

. . . in the Twelfth House

What a lot you're learning about life now, and also about the inner you, thanks to your current mystical and metaphysical insight and understanding. People think you've got the perfect shoulder to cry on, for they need your patience and generosity.

6 Lovers

Divinatory meaning

At first sight, the meaning of this card is obvious - amour! Cupid is about to fire his arrow of amour at the young couple, uniting them in anything from an affectionate friendship to an overwhelming love affair. If you're single then that may not be the case for much longer, or perhaps a relationship that's been a wee bit rocky will grow much stronger. Lovers who've been parted will soon be reunited and a current partnership will go from strength to strength. The Lovers can also signify happiness and harmony with others, perhaps at work or in a family setting.

However, if you look at the card again you'll see it could well have a very different meaning – maybe the couple are trying to face a difficult decision and can't make up their minds? The traditional choice associated with this card is between spiritual and earthly love (perhaps one of the lovers is married to someone else?), but even if that interpretation doesn't apply the decision usually has moral overtones of some sort.

Reversed meaning

There may soon be a parting of the ways, or at least a rift, when this card is reversed. The placing of the card in the spread, and the general feel of the rest of the spread, should say whether the break is temporary or permanent.

Another possible meaning is that you're about to make a mistake in *affaires de coeur*. Maybe you choose a partner for materialistic or mercenary motives, and only realize later that you should have let your heart rule your head, and not the other way round?

Alternatively, you could fall head over heels for someone who's quite unsuitable, already involved with another lover, or who doesn't even know that you exist. Or have you fallen in love with love, so you're seeing things that don't really exist?

. . . in the First House

The time has come to choose between love and loot, but which are you going to plump for? Life is offering you plenty of opportunity for personal satisfaction, so use your current vitality, vibrance and optimism to decide what's right for you.

. . . in the Second House

What's the most important thing in your life? Are materialistic matters the be-all and end-all, do you only feel safe with money in the bank, are art and beauty vital to your happiness or are love and affection top of your list? The time's come to choose.

. . . in the Third House

You're faced with a difficult decision, for you must choose between what you know to be right and what you really want to do. Instead of wavering, wondering and worrying, listen to your conscience and intuition and the right choice will follow.

. . . in the Fourth House

How's the happy home? Is it a haven of harmony or are you caught in the horns of a dilemma that could stir up the very roots of your world? If so, then keep calm and listen to that voice inside you. You'll find you've known the right answer all along.

. . . in the Fifth House

If your love life's giving you gyp then could it be because you've got on your high horse or are standing your ground over an amorous affair? As you now know to your cost, love and pride don't go together. Which one matters most to you?

. . . in the Sixth House

Fed up with the same old routine, wish you could change your job or feeling under the weather? Think about what's really wrong − are you torn between duty and desire, business and pleasure? Then let your intuition guide you to the right decision.

. . . in the Seventh House

What's up with you? Love is supposed to bring a smile to your face but instead you've got a furrowed brow, for you're trying to choose between your conscience and some finely tuned passions. Don't drive your darling demented by delay!

. . . in the Eighth House

Your passion ration's at an all-time high, but that red-hot amour is clouding your brain and preventing you viewing life in a practical and realistic way. Maybe a lover's forcing your hand, making your conscience fight your heart. Which one will win?

. . . in the Ninth House

You're in a right old quandary at the moment, thanks to a question of conscience, troublesome travel plan or religious doubt. The more you stew about it the more muddled and bemused you'll be, so rely on your instincts to give you the answer.

. . . in the Tenth House

Even if you're usually a pillar of propriety and responsibility you feel like turning your back on all that now and doing something different. Your heart wants to go one way and your common sense the other, but which will make you happiest?

. . . in the Eleventh House

If you've been letting your imagination have the upper hand lately or mixing with folk who are way out, wacky or just plain weird, then blending these flights of fancy with your everyday world could be difficult. Should you be more daring, or less?

. . . in the Twelfth House

A romantic reverie's certainly warming the cockles of your heart but it could also be providing you with some pangs of conscience. Perhaps you've got to choose between dreams and reality, but don't make life more difficult than it has to be now.

7 Chariot

Divinatory meaning

This card is full of action, with the young man in the chariot thundering along like a conquering hero. The illustration underlines the main message of this card, which is that you'll succeed if you have faith in yourself and your abilities. The chariot represents the assertiveness, drive and energy that's needed to surmount the obstacles facing you now, and the different coloured horses symbolize your mental and physical abilities which can only be controlled by sheer willpower.

Hard work is in the offing, but if you keep on keeping on and don't give up, the struggle will be worthwhile and the rewards highly satisfying! Take heart that this tricky time certainly won't last forever. Oddly enough, sometimes this card describes events which have just happened, so it may refer to a difficult time that has recently come to an end.

The Chariot can also represent travel, or successful dealings over a car.

Reversed meaning

This card still represents hard slog or an uphill struggle when it's upside down, but unfortunately you seem to be fighting a losing battle at the moment. That may change, of course, with you emerging victorious in the end, but be prepared to put up a fight first. Part of the problem may stem from your indecision or hesitation about how to act for the best, so try to forge ahead with conviction and confidence. The difficulties you're facing may also have been imposed on you by circumstances beyond your control.

Take care that your frustration and anger don't turn into an arrogance that makes you ride roughshod over other folks' feelings, for that could easily happen now.

. . . in the First House

Your winning ways and unbounded enthusiasm mean you'll be able to triumph over almost any adversity or adversary now. The trouble is, you may make such a splash that you're left wondering what to do next! Better let things ride for a wee while.

. . . in the Second House

Congratulations! If it hasn't already happened then you're about to receive some money, but oddly enough that won't be nearly so satisfying as you'd thought. Everything depends on how you use your success, so don't let yourself slip into stagnation.

. . . in the Third House

A difficult debate, discussion or argument has finally been settled with you on the winning side, thanks to your razor-sharp mind. But what happens next? Instead of resting on your laurels it's time to make the most of your other talents too.

. . . in the Fourth House

Been waging a battle about a domestic difficulty or caught in a conflict with kith and kin? Well, victory will soon be yours and how sweet it will be, but it could leave you feeling let down or lethargic. Why not relax at home for a while? You deserve it!

. . . in the Fifth House

You're riding on the crest of a wave, enjoying the fruits of success and basking in the adoration and admiration of loved ones. Have fun whilst it lasts but don't get so carried away in the present that you forget to plan for the future.

. . . in the Sixth House

The sweet smell of success makes all workaday dealings a positive pleasure, for you're really revealing your true talents and attributes at last. Pat yourself on the back, then start your next project pronto whilst applause still rings in your ears.

. . . in the Seventh House

One-to-one affairs are ace! Partners know where they stand for you've brought peace and harmony to all your relationships. Wedding bells could chime soon, unless you're already part of a happy couple, of course! Enjoy yourself!

. . . in the Eighth House

Passions have been running high lately but all that emotion has certainly paid off in some wonderful ways. Even so, love isn't the only thing in life so think about other important topics too, such as business, boodle and how you feel deep down inside.

. . . in the Ninth House

A recent triumph has left you feeling exuberant and expansive, especially if it was connected with distant lands, an environmental or intellectual matter. Thinking of taking a long trip? Then do it now whilst travel plans look so good.

. . . in the Tenth House

Your career certainly seems to have been bolstered by your recent success, or soon will be! You're on to a winner so bask in the spotlight of success whilst it lasts, but don't ignore other areas of your life that could do with some attention too.

. . . in the Eleventh House

A pet plan or project for the future is about to come up trumps, especially if you had a bit of a battle getting it off the ground. You'll be the centre of attention, and about time too! Why not celebrate by going out on the town with a few friends?

. . . in the Twelfth House

Understanding ourselves and coping with our hidden emotions can be hard, but you've passed with flying colours! Now that you've come to terms with the fears and phobias inside you it's time to deal with folk who've been playing on your feelings.

8 *Justice*

Divinatory meaning

As its name suggests, this card represents justice in all its forms. Here is the classic figure of Justice (in Greek mythology she was Astraea, goddess of justice) with her scales to help her to determine right from wrong and her shining double-edged sword. She is urging you to be reasonable and impartial, like herself.

When this card appears it may well mean that a legal wrangle has a favourable outcome, especially if it falls in the ninth house (which rules legal matters) of the horoscope spread, but it has a much wider interpretation than that.

Any decisions taken now that affect you will be made fairly and rationally, and with your best interests at heart. If you're involved in an argument then a third person may intervene and pour oil on troubled waters. Order will also be restored to any situations or circumstances that are chaotic or confused.

This is a good card to choose if you're about to embark on a new enterprise or venture, or if you'll soon be pairing up with someone, because it shows that everyone involved will act in an honest and fair fashion.

Reversed meaning

Sadly, justice may not be the outcome when this card is reversed. If you are involved in a legal battle then it could go against you, or at least take a long time to be sorted out.

In everyday affairs you may soon suffer from someone's unfair or unprovoked bad behaviour, so be warned! It's not a good time to confide or trust in folk either, for they could use that information against you in the future.

If you're applying for a new job or promotion then don't be surprised if you're overlooked or ignored.

On the other hand, of course, if you've been acting in an underhand or dishonest way then you're about to get your come-uppance!

. . . in the First House

Don't worry if you've been misunderstood or misrepresented recently, for it's time to clear the air and show your true self at last. Folk will soon realize they haven't given you a chance to make the most of your abilities, so off you go!

. . . in the Second House

Money matters have been a wee bit tricky lately, making you feel aggrieved and resentful. Maybe someone's sharp practice did you down, but you'll soon get what's rightfully yours. Just make sure your own actions are above-board, otherwise you'll pay the price!

. . . in the Third House

You've been brimming with brainwaves and inspired ideas recently, but has someone tried to steal your limelight or claim your concepts for their own? Well, justice is about to be done, so burnish your brain cells ready for your next tour de force!

. . . in the Fourth House

Has someone tried to pull the wool over your eyes in a domestic matter, or are you nursing some old scores you want to settle? Then keep calm, for everything's about to come out in the wash. Concentrate instead on strengthening your family ties.

. . . in the Fifth House

Feeling hard done by, ignored by loved ones or as though a creative concern's going nowhere fast? Then sit tight and do nowt, for all your problems are about to disappear, letting your personality and true talents shine through at long last!

. . . in the Sixth House

All that hard work, all that dedication, but what do you have to show for it? If that's the way you feel now then you can be sure the scales of justice will soon swing your way. Your honesty will pay dividends in the end, so just let matters take their course.

. . . in the Seventh House

Has a partner done you down, acted behind your back or been less than honest? Then instead of plotting your revenge or giving them a dose of their own medicine, stick to the straight and narrow in the knowledge that the truth will soon be told.

. . . in the Eighth House

Skulduggery, double-dealing and deception are all around you now, so let's hope you're not the one stirring up trouble. You may long to get your own back but that will only make matters worse. Sit tight, say nowt, and justice will soon be done!

. . . in the Ninth House

Travel broadens the mind, but it's got yours in a right old muddle recently thanks to someone's slip-ups, secrecy or matters beyond your control. Well, forget about retribution and try a little patience instead, then everything will work itself out.

. . . in the Tenth House

How frustrated can you get? You're trying to make your mark on the world and receive the recognition you deserve, but someone or something is standing in your way. Calm down, 'cos all those injustices are about to be resolved in your favour.

. . . in the Eleventh House

Getting up in arms about social injustices or a friend's bad behaviour will do you no good at all now, so don't waste your time and energy trying. Instead, be as honest as possible and be comforted with the knowledge that all will soon be resolved.

. . . in the Twelfth House

The scales of justice will soon be tipping in your favour, so stop worrying and fretting about misfortunes or unfairnesses that you couldn't fight even if you tried. You know this in your heart of hearts, so let your intuitions be your guide.

9 Hermit

Divinatory meaning

It's time to withdraw far from the madding crowd and to ponder on problems or perplexities in peace when The Hermit appears in a spread. The illustration on the card shows a wise-looking man emerging from his cave, holding a lamp to guide his way. If you imagine the cave symbolizing his unconscious, and the lamp as his intellect and constant search for knowledge, you'll see he's trying to use his mind to see his way forward. In other words, this isn't a time for action but one of careful thought, of mulling things over and weighing up the pros and cons. If you must make an important decision now, then you'll soon realize that the answer to your problem lies deep within you.

Another meaning of this card is wanting to escape from other people for a while, perhaps to recover from an illness or just to have some time to yourself. You prefer your own company at the moment.

Reversed meaning

Isolation, depression and loneliness are signified when this card is reversed, but often they're of your own making. If you're in trouble or going through a bad patch now then you'd rather struggle on by yourself than accept someone's offer of help or support. That's all very well, but try not to antagonize or annoy well-meaning folk just for the sake of it. Alternatively, you may have recently been bereaved, divorced or heart-broken, and want to lick your wounds in peace for a while. If you're hoping that a break in a love affair's only temporary, a reversed Hermit when backed up by other cards may suggest otherwise.

. . . in the First House

Self-analysis is one thing but endlessly cogitating about your every move is quite another, and that's the danger now. It's good to try to understand yourself, but the best way to do that is by relating to others, so don't keep yourself to yourself!

. . . in the Second House

Money is uppermost in your mind, whether you're rolling in loot or wondering how to make ends meet. The question is whether you're paying too much attention to materialistic matters or making good pecuniary plans for a firm financial future?

. . . in the Third House

Having some time to yourself will be invaluable now, but don't hide away from everyone for too long. It's a grand time to escape from the pressures of everyday life, put pen to paper or just indulge in some quiet cogitation and contemplation.

. . . in the Fourth House

Locking yourself away in the comfort and security of your own abode is just what you want now, especially if you can forge closer links with kith and kin. But don't go overboard and shut yourself off from the rest of the world!

. . . in the Fifth House

You're torn in two directions, trying to decide whether to get out and about or disappear into a thoughtful world of your own. Well, spending some time locked in serious thought and getting to know yourself will pay dividends in coming weeks.

. . . in the Sixth House

All the signs show you need to do some serious thinking, especially if you're wondering whether to reorganize part of your life. If not, subconscious worries could surface in weird worries about a health or work matter, so don your thinking cap!

. . . in the Seventh House

Meditation is the key to happiness now, for this is your chance to improve all one-to-one affairs by thinking things through and mulling over people's motives. You'll be able to gain fresh insights into partners and valuable understanding of loved ones.

. . . in the Eighth House

It looks as though your heart is ruling your head at the moment, especially where intimate affairs or official money matters are concerned. However, you must get your hot-blooded feelings into order and work out priorities before you do sommat rash.

. . . in the Ninth House

What a philosopher you are at the moment! Even so, you should sift through your thoughts first and separate the wheat from the chaff before letting your ideas loose on the waiting world. Planning a trip? Then think hard before committing yourself.

. . . in the Tenth House

Professional or prestigious pursuits are never far from your thoughts now, but if you're honest you'll admit you're not quite sure which direction you want to take. Don't make a move until you've worked out pros and cons and know what you want.

. . . in the Eleventh House

Soul-searching is on the cards now, for the more you meditate and cogitate the more you'll learn – and change into a more spiritual you. Thinking of taking up a new hobby? Then yoga or anything linked with mystical matters could be just the ticket.

. . . in the Twelfth House

Don't worry if you've had some odd dreams lately – it's just your psyche trying to tell you there's more to life than meets the eye. Thinking deep thoughts will improve your knowledge of yourself, and heighten your perceptions and insights too.

10 Wheel of Fortune

Divinatory meaning

This is the luckiest card in the pack, for it shows that the fates are with you (you can see the good luck charms and other fateful symbols scattered about the card). The illustration on the card shows the Wheel of Fortune, which is always turning. It looks rather like a roulette wheel (except it is marked with the glyphs for the 12 zodiac signs) and at the moment it is coming up trumps for you, ensuring good times are on the way; a turn for the better. Better make the most of them whilst they last!

Big changes are on the way in whichever area of the spread this card falls, and it's up to you to turn them to your advantage whenever possible. Opportunities will arise now that should be jumped at, and plans and projects could also develop in a wonderful way.

If you've been faced with difficulties lately then expect them to disappear, or at least get better, now. An unexpected event or encounter could prove to be a real godsend, perhaps introducing you to someone special or putting you on the path to prominence or prosperity.

Reversed meaning

Sadly, the Wheel of Fortune has turned (what goes up must come down) and is now dispensing difficulties and disappointments instead of good fortune. Setbacks or strife could strike like bolts from the blue now, or you might be let down when you least expect it; a turn for the worse. The area of the spread in which this card falls will tell you a lot about where the problems and pitfalls will arise, so you can take precautions if necessary and be better prepared. For instance, it's a good idea to tidy up any loose ends in that area of life before you're caught out. When things do go wrong, you can either let them get you down and feel sorry for yourself, or see them as a challenge that you can and will overcome. Which is it to be?

. . . in the First House

You're bubbling away with such enthusiasm and abundant energy that you'll draw all sorts of fortunate folk into your orbit if you play your cards right and make the most of your charm and charisma. Lady Luck is certainly smiling on you!

. . . in the Second House

Fate is ringing the financial changes for you and bringing boodle your way, but don't let your impatience upset the apple cart. Fortune is with you in wheeling and dealing too, so be sure to to grasp opportunities the moment they arise.

. . . in the Third House

Put pen to paper now and it could be the start of something big! Whether you're writing your novel, dashing off chatty letters or entering competitions, communications will pay dividends. You may also get a lucky break or some good news that changes your life!

. . . in the Fourth House

Happy changes are in the offing on the home front. If you're house hunting you could find the perfect place, but redecorating will go well too. Kith and kin may also benefit from your good fortune and family matters will be cosy and warm.

. . . in the Fifth House

Dame Destiny's smiling on you at the moment, so make the most of this terrific time by letting your super personality shine through and attract influential or friendly folk to your side. Blow your own trumpet and get yourself noticed now!

. . . in the Sixth House

It's all change on the work front, bringing opportunities to show what sterling stuff you're made of. You're dedicated and perfectionist in all you tackle now, and that's just what bosses and clients want! There's good news about a medical matter too.

. . . in the Seventh House

Partnerships of all persuasions have hit the jackpot, ensuring an idyllic interlude when you'll get on great with everyone you meet. As for amour, well it's all around you now, so prepare to reach new heights of bliss with a very special sweetheart!

. . . in the Eighth House

Trust in your hunches and you won't go far wrong. No one can pull the wool over your eyes at the moment, making it a fine time to pursue matters connected with the taxman or large financial institutions. Your passion ration's also on the up, so enjoy!

. . . in the Ninth House

Cosmopolitan concerns look lucky, and anything connected with travel or foreign lands will go well - but only if you grab opportunities the instant they appear and don't let life pass you by. If you fancy a flutter then you could come up trumps!

. . . in the Tenth House

Take the initiative, seize on your good fortune and you'll soon be heading straight for the top! Promotion, prestige and applause are yours for the taking now, but don't forget you'll have to work hard even if chances do seem to land in your lap.

. . . in the Eleventh House

Been nurturing a long-term plan or wish that's slightly eccentric or unusual? Then don't delay any longer, for it's an ideal opportunity to get it off the drawing board and into action. Be sociable too for friends could bring luck your way now.

. . . in the Twelfth House

Make the most of your perceptions and instincts and you won't put a foot wrong. You're at your best getting in touch with your inner self now, which could lead to important and far-reaching changes to your emotions and a much better life ahead!

11 *Strength*

Divinatory meaning

This is one of those tarot cards with a straightforward meaning, saying that you should be strong in whichever situation arises now. In the illustration, the young woman is easily able to handle the lion, showing that willpower and determination can work better than brute strength. The message of the card is that, whatever happens, you must bring out your innate perseverance, patience and courage, and be brave in the face of adversity.

The lion illustrated on the card has two meanings. It may represent events or encounters that are about to happen to you, and which you might have a hard time dealing with, or it can symbolize the inner temptations or weaknesses that you must control and combat if you're going to succeed now. Either way, you'll come through with flying colours, and may even discover depths and strengths in your personality you never knew you had.

If this card appears when you've been ill or depressed, or have had a run of bad luck, it shows things will soon get better.

Reversed meaning

Just as this card shows strength when upright, so it represents weakness when it's reversed. For example, it might indicate that a bad bout of ill health is on the way, or that you'll find it hard to shake off a current ailment or illness. If you're already feeling fed up then that sorry state could continue for some time to come. Alternatively, maybe you'll finally give into a temptation that you've struggled against but can no longer resist, such as taking up cigarettes again or abandoning your diet? Your willpower is low or lost.

You might be faced with a task or responsibility that you think is beyond you and so not even try to tackle it. Then, instead of using your energy to have a go and see how much you can achieve, you'll waste it by worrying and feeling guilty about your failings!

. . . in the First House

It's one thing to be determined and know what you want, but quite another to be so pushy that you turn folk against you, and that's the danger you're facing now. Take things at a steady pace and the sheer force of your personality will open doors for you.

. . . in the Second House

You're holding all the cards in cash concerns, so making lots of loot now won't be a problem. What you should worry about is letting all that power get the better of you. You can take a risk and come out on top but give other folk a chance too.

. . . in the Third House

Winning debates or talking people round is easy now, for you exude such power and authority no one's going to argue with you. That doesn't mean you can't make mistakes, though! You can certainly get your own way by force, but is that the best policy?

. . . in the Fourth House

You're a real tower of strength in your own domestic domain now, and kith and kin will let you call the shots, even if they think you're wrong. But be diplomatic, and don't expect to get your own way all the time, for this powerful patch won't last!

. . . in the Fifth House

Being the centre of attention suits you down to the ground at the moment, but don't fall into the trap of taking your popularity for granted or letting your pride take the upper hand. Enjoy your current charisma with loved ones but keep on an even keel.

. . . in the Sixth House

Work finds you in a forceful position and able to organize others into doing what you want, but that could be dangerous unless you use some common sense and stop yourself acting like a petty dictator. So make good use of your strength but be fair.

. . . in the Seventh House

You're the boss where relationships are concerned now, and it'll be only too easy to force partners into accepting what you want rather than talk things through rationally and quietly. Try not to give into the temptation, or issue ultimata!

. . . in the Eighth House

Power's emanating from every pore now, but are you sure that's such a good thing? Railroading close companions or financial associates into doing your bidding is easy as pie, but success may not taste so sweet when your actions rebound on you later!

. . . in the Ninth House

Putting across your ideas can be fun, but trying to change the world single-handed is another matter. Calm down! People will listen to you now so why are you being so forceful and dogmatic? Being in a strong position doesn't always mean being right!

. . . in the Tenth House

Sheer strength of will can help you to clinch important deals or bulldoze through opposition at work, but is that really the best way to reach your goals? Instead of making some potential enemies why not put your energy and power to positive use?

. . . in the Eleventh House

You're the life and soul of the social scene now and number one on everyone's popularity polls, but don't push your luck by believing that what you say goes or ordering everyone else around. Some inventive ideas could really pay off.

. . . in the Twelfth House

Anyone in trouble will head straight for you now, for you've got the sensitivity and sympathy they need. What they won't realize is that by helping them you'll be helping yourself to tune into other people's feelings and increase your own understanding.

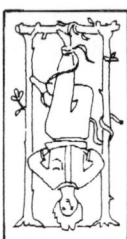

12 *Hanged Man*

Divinatory meaning

This is one of the cards that looks full of doom and gloom, but don't worry because it isn't nearly as bad as it seems and can even be very positive. After all, the man is hanging from his foot, not his neck (this is the only card with a figure on it that is the right way up when the figure is upside-down!), and he is definitely still alive. In fact, the tarot shows him hanging upside down to indicate he's viewing his life from an unusual or altered angle, which is traditionally in a more spiritual and less materialistic manner than normal. He may also be in limbo between one important event and another, or about to change his mind about something.

Not surprisingly, some sort of self-sacrifice is usually indicated by this card, so look carefully at the area of the spread in which it falls. Maybe you'll be offered a more satisfying job but will have to take a hefty pay cut as a result?

You might also have an experience of great personal value that involves some sort of sacrifice which other folk wouldn't put up with. Something that seems disastrous may also happen, but you'll soon spot the silver lining to this current cloud.

Reversed meaning

Beware of making needless or useless sacrifices now, and be especially wary of acting the martyr or giving in to self-pitying or negative actions. You may think you're powerless to change or improve a difficult situation or circumstance but are you so sure? Maybe it's easier or less frightening to put up with the problems than to try to change them, or perhaps you enjoy being on the receiving end of everyone's sympathy and attention?

Occasionally, a reversed Hanged Man can indicate someone who's suffering from an addiction (perhaps to drink or drugs), has lost all grip on reality or is indulging in negative escapism. If other cards also suggest it, this card can even indicate suicide.

. . . in the First House

There's no doubt you've made sacrifices in your personal life lately, but you know in your heart of hearts how necessary they were. The experiences you're going through now are helping you to learn about yourself, so a wiser and renewed you can emerge.

. . . in the Second House

The financial hardships you've endured in the past are for a purpose, I promise, because they're teaching you the true value of material things and helping you to put your pecuniary position into perspective. You'll be a lot wiser at the end of it!

. . . in the Third House

Your brain's working on overdrive, making you eager to add to your store of knowledge. A whole new world could open up, so consolidate your ideas and concentrate on one thing at a time. You'll soon be amazed at your own resilience.

. . . in the Fourth House

Loved ones are on your mind now, especially if you think it's time to make some changes to your domestic set-up, but don't act too hastily. Take your time and let a new closeness and deep loving understanding develop between you and loved ones.

. . . in the Fifth House

Calm, cool and collected, that's how you seem on the surface, but deep down you're preparing for the future, for you know folk will have a shock when the new you appears. Your love life has led to sacrifices in the past, but they'll soon pay dividends.

. . . in the Sixth House

Life isn't always a bed of roses, as you know to your cost, but the good news is that all your past hard work is finally starting to pay off. At last you can explore new areas, whether in work or health matters, so start planning now!

. . . in the Seventh House

One-to-one affairs haven't always been easy, particularly if you've put a partner's needs before your own. But now things are changing, for you're viewing all your relationships from a new and inspired angle. It's time to learn from experience.

. . . in the Eighth House

Have you often been a slave to your desires or felt yourself propelled by passion? Well, all that's about to alter, for you're entering a new phase when you can be more objective and rational about those seething emotions. You'll be wiser as a result.

. . . in the Ninth House

Grab every experience going now, for your approach to life is becoming broader with each day that dawns. You're much more adventurous, enquiring, inquisitive and even philosophical than before, so come on, discover the world and the new you too!

. . . in the Tenth House

Everyone's made mistakes in the past and you're no exception, but now's the time to learn from those errors, put them in perspective and apply them to your future prospects. Grand opportunities are on the way in business and career concerns!

. . . in the Eleventh House

Put on your thinking cap where future plans are concerned, for there may be plenty of room for improvement before they're ready for lift-off. Don't be afraid to eliminate anything that's holding you back – and that includes your friends!

. . . in the Twelfth House

Stop ignoring your hunches, flashes of inspiration or intuition and start to listen to your subconscious! The more you trust in it, the more accurate it'll become, leading to a much wiser, experienced and perceptive you. The benefits will be boundless!

13 Death

Divinatory meaning

People unused to the tarot can find this card very upsetting at first, but it very rarely means a physical death. Instead, the roses growing out of the skull signify important, positive and far-reaching changes and transformations that are on the way – you are reaching the end of one stage in your life and are about to embark on another. The skull on the card symbolizes the death of the old, and the beautiful red roses represent the subsequent birth and growth of something new and flourishing.

You may well be expecting the changes that are about to take place, although they won't all plain sailing. It might be painful or difficult to cope at times, especially if a close relationship is coming to an end or if you always find it hard to accept changes in your world, but rest assured that what's happening now will lead to the birth of a brand new you. You will emerge stronger than ever! Rebirth and regeneration sum up this important card.

Reversed meaning

If you've been digging your heels in, resisting the inevitable or trying to prevent important alterations taking place in your world, then you're on a losing wicket. Big changes are on the way whether you like it or not! Standing in the path of progress, even if that's not the way you see it, will only make you more miserable and confused in the long run, so try to give in gracefully. If a relationship is drawing to an upsetting close then resist the temptation to cling on to your partner, for that's the way to lose them forever now. Any difficulties or problems you've tried to brush under the carpet may also come to light now in an embarrassing or unpleasant way, so watch your step! Fate, destiny, kismet – you name it, but this card reversed tells you you're powerless to resist or fight the inevitable.

. . . in the First House

All change! You need to cut your losses, clear the decks and start again, and if you're honest with yourself you'll know a complete overhaul is long overdue. Instead of clinging to the past with all it's problems, it's time to look to the future!

. . . in the Second House

Watch your step in all money matters for the cards suggest you're on the wrong track or about to come a cropper. Try to stash away some cash for that rainy day, but choose a safe and secure savings scheme. You can't afford to take any financial risks now.

. . . in the Third House

If you've been pushing a pile of paperwork to one side or postponing important errands then prepare to be caught out! Why not learn your lesson and tackle chores in good time from now on? You could hear news now that completely alters your thinking.

. . . in the Fourth House

Drastic action is needed on the home front, for you can't kid yourself any longer that everything's hunky dory. Maybe it's time to live in the present, not the past, or have a showdown with a recalcitrant relative, but act you must – and quickly!

. . . in the Fifth House

Just like a chrysalis, you're facing a total transformation in your life, when the old you will be reborn into someone stronger and wiser. Altering the way you express yourself and react to loved ones is the first step, so take it now.

. . . in the Sixth House

You need to take yourself in hand before matters are taken out of your control. If your health isn't A1 then seek medical advice or embark on a fitness campaign that will revitalize you, or make changes to improve your job. A new dawn beckons!

. . . in the Seventh House

Life is all about change and growth, so be prepared for major alterations in your one-to-one affairs. Whether you reach a new understanding with a partner or sever a tie totally, out of bad will come good. You're moving from the dark into the light.

. . . in the Eighth House

Prepare for a time of intense emotions and profound passions in intimate affairs. Perhaps it's a parting of the ways with your other half, loss of a loved one, a crisis over a sexual problem or turmoil in shared money matters? Look, listen and learn!

. . . in the Ninth House

If you're all set to fly off into the wide blue yonder then don't be surprised if your plans are cancelled due to circumstances beyond your control. Events or experiences that take place now will force you to revise your beliefs, with rewarding results.

. . . in the Tenth House

If your aims and ambitions are stuck in limbo then maybe it's because you're barking up the wrong tree? Thinking things through will reveal where you've gone awry and how to get back on course, so be brave and strike out in new directions!

. . . in the Eleventh House

Take a good look at the social side of your life. Do you like what you see or have you spotted some problems? Maybe you've lost touch with your friends or are mixing with folk you don't really like? Whatever's wrong, this is your chance to start afresh.

. . . in the Twelfth House

Are you feeling confused, unhappy or do you want to hide away by yourself? Then you must delve deep into your mind, look your innermost fears and phobias in the face and prune away emotional dead wood. You'll emerge relieved, renewed and reborn!

14 Temperance

Divinatory meaning

The illustration on this card shows an angel pouring a steady stream of liquid from one cup to another without spilling any of it, and this symbolizes moderation, discipline and frugality. The liquid represents the essence of life, with the past flowing peacefully and easily into the present and the future. When this card appears in a reading it indicates a person who is resourceful, responsible and efficient, and whose tact, caution and perseverance enables them to control their emotions and cope with whatever problems and pitfalls life places in their path.

If money is tight at the moment, you'll be able to manage by budgeting accordingly and living well within your means (shown by the careful way the liquid is being poured from one cup to the other). You'll also have a strong spiritual sense of satisfaction now that will spur you on if times get tough. In fact, whatever area of your life is affected by this card, you'll be able to take a balanced and moderate approach in which common sense wins the day!

Reversed meaning

If you've been overdoing *la dolce vita* lately, then this card is telling you in no uncertain terms to pay more attention to your health! Maybe you should cut down on the grub and grog, embark on an exercise regime or go on a diet? Your waistline and your wallet will both benefit!

Impatience, restlessness or a lack of experience may make it hard for you to get on well with others at the moment, or perhaps you make heavy weather out of social situations that are usually easy and enjoyable. Even if you're normally tactful you could drop a few clangers now, or act out of character by doing something silly or stupid. Try to be more aware of your actions now and think before you speak!

. . . in the First House

Calm down! There's no doubting your current energy and enthusiasm, but you may not realize how overwhelming and off-putting it can be for others. Instead of charging ahead without thinking, temper your actions and stop coming on so strong.

. . . in the Second House

Throwing your money around like confetti may be good fun but if you do it for too long you'll be up a financial gum tree. Instead, why not work out a sensible budget you can stick to, or investigate a savings scheme that'll bring you a nice nest-egg?

. . . in the Third House

Stop jumping in at the deep end! You've only too eager to swing into action or speak your mind now but sooner or later it'll land you in hot water. Instead, try to tone down your activities, do some hard thinking and let others get a word in edgeways!

. . . in the Fourth House

Hold it! It's time to take stock of your domestic domain. Instead of rushing in where angels fear to tread you should consult kith and kin over decisions that involve you all, or weigh up the pros and cons before making major changes to your way of life.

. . . in the Fifth House

Make moderation in all things your motto now, otherwise you could rub folk up the wrong way or be accused of singing your own praises too loudly. Think first, and you'll strike the right note when it comes to advertising your abilities and attributes.

. . . in the Sixth House

Hard work's all very well but you can't let it affect your health. Instead of trying to do everything at once you must tackle tasks in their order of priority. So start being kind to yourself and have a well-earned breather!

. . . in the Seventh House

You're tackling one-to-one affairs like a bull at a gate now, coming on strong and scared to let folk out of your sight. Carry on like this and you'll frighten everyone off, so be a wee bit cool and detached and let 'em chase after you. They soon will!

. . . in the Eighth House

Talk about hot and heavy! You must get a good grip on yourself before your seething emotions boil over into jealousy or even revenge. Shared financial affairs need a cautious approach too, especially if you're dealing with officious officials.

. . . in the Ninth House

Are you sure everyone wants to hear all your viewpoints and ideas, or do they even have a choice? If you've just discovered a new belief or creed then beware of shoving it down other folk's throats! Travel plans may have to be postponed.

. . . in the Tenth House

Before you start planning your next boardroom coup or move up the ladder of success, check the facts, otherwise you could come unstuck or be left with egg on your face. A parental or prestigious problem needs a softly softly approach.

. . . in the Eleventh House

If you've been burning the candle at both ends or socializing till all hours then maybe you need to curb things for a while? A particular friendship may also be getting out of hand, so put the brakes on now before it's too late. Go carefully!

. . . in the Twelfth House

Stop anticipating problems and worrying about things that may never happen! Instead, get to the bottom of anxieties you're trying to push to the back of your mind and then take each day as it comes. Don't trouble trouble till trouble troubles you!

15 Devil

Divinatory meaning

This is one of the cards that can strike fear in the hearts of folk when it appears in a spread, but it's not as bad or as sinister as it seems. In many packs the Devil is chained up in some way, indicating an enslavement or bondage to material matters − on this card, the Devil is surrounded by flames, to suggest you're being plagued by oppressive people, problems or worries that are looming over you and won't give you any peace. You may even feel dominated and ruled by them, but isn't there something you can do, however small, to escape or alleviate your current crisis? Sticking to a stagnant status quo just because you don't want to make a fuss or rock the boat will backfire in the long run, for you'll feel full of frustration, resentment and anger as a result. Temptation through Mammon.

The area of the spread in which this card falls will reveal where the problems lie − perhaps in persisting in a partnership that only brings tears and torment, or following a way of life that's steeped in materialistic or mercenary motives? You might also soon be involved in a torrid emotional encounter which revolves around some steamy sex.

Reversed meaning

There are two meanings to this card when it's reversed. Firstly, it's warning you not to get involved with folk who are negative, nefarious or who dabble in the darker side of spirituality. Beware of anything to do with black magic or other activities that your conscience tells you are wrong. Stick to the straight and narrow and don't get involved in anything underhand or dishonest, no matter how tempting it may seem.

Alternatively, the oppressive or depressive situations that are weighing so heavily on you now will soon pass. Perhaps you've finally realized that you can do something positive to change your current circumstances? You're easily tempted off the straight and narrow path − and would even sell your best friend down the river to get what you want.

. . . in the First House

Keep a tight rein on your temper now otherwise you'll have to contend with anything from rows to huge personality clashes. Maybe you should come to terms with what's really wrong instead of letting rip for no good reason at all? Keep your cool!

. . . in the Second House

Stick to the straight and narrow in all money matters for this is no time to run risks. You shouldn't lend anything you can't afford to lose, as you may not get it back. Watch your spending too, as extravagance is only a wallet away now!

. . . in the Third House

Think before you speak, otherwise what seems harmless to you may be misconstrued by one with an axe to grind. Don't put in writing anything you might regret, either. Watch your step if you're dashing hither and thither for you could be accident-prone now.

. . . in the Fourth House

Steer clear of any wheeling and dealing associated with your abode or you'll hit problems galore. Tread carefully with kith and kin, especially if one of you is bad tempered or acting out of character. Make sure your home's burglar-proof now.

. . . in the Fifth House

Dealings with dear ones may be anything but easy at the moment, thanks to a child's wayward actions or a loved one who's cutting up rough or deliberately making life a misery for you. Go easy if you're out on the town, for you may over-indulge.

. . . in the Sixth House

Keep a close eye on workaday and medical matters, for it seems you've got yourself into a right old muddle. Maybe you're fighting a lost cause at work, have reached a dead end or are feeling under the weather, but don't let it prey on your mind.

. . . in the Seventh House

Someone's playing games, but the question is who? Partnerships of all persuasions are prone to deception and difficulties now, so be prepared for any eventuality. Honesty is definitely your best policy, for lying or cheating will cause chaos in the future.

. . . in the Eighth House

Let your emotions get the better of you and you'll be skating on very thin ice indeed. Guard against arousing possessiveness or envy in your other half, or rising to the bait yourself, and proceed with considerable caution in all joint money matters.

. . . in the Ninth House

Off on your travels? Then double-check timetables and insurances, and don't trust everyone you meet on the way. Someone could convince you that their belief, religion or cause is the one for you, but beware of being brainwashed or browbeaten.

. . . in the Tenth House

Keeping your head down is your best bet in all business and career concerns at the moment, 'cos making a name for yourself is anything but easy now. Someone may be keeping you in the dark or trying to trip you up, or is it you who's up to no good?

. . . in the Eleventh House

A so-called friend could try to lead you astray, but don't be swayed by their sweet talk into doing anything you're unhappy about. Steer clear of any unruly or suspect social settings for the moment, otherwise you could be asking for trouble.

. . . in the Twelfth House

It would be the easiest thing in the world now to get mixed up in something slightly shady, shifty or secret, but you must resist the temptation at all costs. Be choosy about what you read or watch too, for anything unpleasant could prey on your mind.

16 Tower

Divinatory meaning

This isn't a good card to have in a spread, especially if it appears repeatedly in someone's readings, as you will see from the illustration. A tower, which represents your previous knowledge and beliefs, is being blasted by an unexpected bolt of lightning, which signifies a clean break with the past. However, it has positive effects if you're in a negative situation you want out of − and fast!

In other words, you're about to undergo an accident, encounter or experience that'll have a profound effect on your life and ensure that things are never the same again. You'll be brought up short and life could seem very negative and bleak at the time, but you can rest assured that once the dust has settled you'll realize that out of bad has come plenty of good. Be prepared to view people in a new light that's stripped of the illusions or delusions you've had about them, and also to be more honest and objective about your own motives and needs. Your strength of character is about to be put to the test!

Reversed meaning

The Tower is still an unpleasant card when it's reversed, but it usually indicates that the calamity or catastrophe has already arrived and may even have been going on for some time. All the more reason, then, to find ways of coping with this problematic patch once and for all. However, you may be so depressed and downcast that you just can't be bothered to make the necessary effort. If so, try to fight against such a negative attitude because you can climb out of this slough of despond if you really want to. The problems themselves won't go away yet, but at least you can change your attitude towards them so they're easier to live with. Do not despair, but always remember with this card that when something appears at its most safe and solid, that's when it's actually at its most vulnerable. Change and upheaval come when they're least expected.

. . . in the First House

Sweeping changes are on the way, so grab this opportunity to embark on a new chapter in the story of your life. Adopting a different, more positive, approach will help, for this is an exciting chance to rebuild your world for the better.

. . . in the Second House

If you've always lived on credit or spent what you haven't got then you're about to face the hour of reckoning! Seek the advice of financial folk if you're suddenly left high and dry, then don't be too proud to learn from your monetary mistakes.

. . . in the Third House

A bolt from the blue is soon to strike your everyday world. Maybe there'll be a rift with a neighbour, news about a close relative or problems in your community, but whatever it is will lead to the birth of a brand new you.

. . . in the Fourth House

Domestic disruption is in the offing, so stand by for a testing time in your home affairs. It's bound to be a poignant period, but don't cling on to the past or stand in the way of change, or you'll just make matters worse in the long run.

. . . in the Fifth House

Hold on to your heartstrings, for cataclysmic events are about to have an overwhelming and profound effect on your emotions. A loving liaison could end overnight or a creative dream may be shattered, but good will triumph in the end.

. . . in the Sixth House

There are big changes on the horizon in the way you earn your daily bread, but even if they're hard to take at the time you'll realize how valuable they've been once they're over. Look after your health, and don't let odd ailments go unchecked.

. . . in the Seventh House

A new broom is soon to sweep clean all your relationships, getting rid of any partnerships that are past their prime and forcing you to re-evaluate and reconsider all your one-to-one affairs. It won't be easy, but the rewards will be rich.

. . . in the Eighth House

Official or shared money matters could be a cause for concern, especially if you've been leaving things to chance or letting them slide. Clear up those loose ends before they trip you up. Don't let a jealous streak ruin a close relationship.

. . . in the Ninth House

The more open-minded and objective you are, the better you'll fare during the coming disruptive time, for all your creeds and convictions are about to put to the acid test. You'll emerge on the other side transformed and with a new design for living.

. . . in the Tenth House

Don't take anything for granted in professional, parental or prestigious pursuits, for even the best laid plans could come to naught now thanks to massive alterations and disruptions. They'll be in your own best interests, but don't expect an easy ride.

. . . in the Eleventh House

If a hope or dream's been looking like pie in the sky, then the events that overtake you now will reveal where you've gone wrong and put you back on the path to success. A showdown with a friend will be traumatic, but good in the long run.

. . . in the Twelfth House

Circumstances beyond your control are forcing you to face a host of worries, fears and neuroses that you've been ignoring. Only by being honest with yourself and acknowledging faults as well as virtues can you be rejuvenated and reborn.

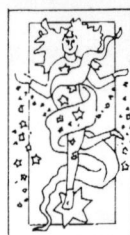

Divinatory meaning

This is a lovely card to have in any spread, because it represents hope, happiness and optimism. Think of it as wishing upon a star and having your dream come true! The name of the card refers to the star followed by the Magi when Christ was born. Traditionally, the maiden on the card is Proserpina, the daughter of Ceres by Jupiter, and so beautiful that she was carried off to the underworld by its king, Pluto.

The Star is an especially beneficial card if you've been ill, struggling in some way or going through a terrible time, because it's promising you peace and a complete recovery from the ills that have assailed you. If you're still suffering from problems then some unexpected blessings could arrive just when they're needed and transform your world for the better. Public recognition is also predicted by this card.

Although this card can mean that long-awaited rewards and recognition are finally on their way to you, it may also indicate that a mundane matter will be imbued with extra importance and significance now. Educational or creative concerns will also benefit from this card, and if it falls in the love area of a spread then fairy-tale romance and heartfelt affection are on the way. Wonderful!

Reversed meaning

This is such a favourable card that its meaning is scarcely changed when it's reversed. The only possible problems may be pessimism, perhaps unfounded, about a new project, paramour or partner. Maybe your innate insecurity or past experiences make it hard for you to believe in the joy and happiness that surround you now, or you're frightened to grab the opportunities that arise in case they vanish before your very eyes? Well, trust in your good fortune and enjoy this propitious period while it lasts! The worst it can indicate is a fall from grace or favour when reversed.

. . . in the First House

Optimism will pay dividends now, so let your true personality shine forth and act like a beacon to others. Make the most of your current energy and enthusiasm, rely on your personal magnetism and all your dealings will be starred for success.

. . . in the Second House

Money matters will rise or fall according to your attitude of mind, so be as positive and optimistic as possible. Learning from past pecuniary mistakes will also stand you in super stead for the future, so don't let all that experience go to waste.

. . . in the Third House

Best foot forward! Whatever you tackle will profit from an enthusiastic and positive approach, so keep smiling and you'll make great progress. Looking on the bright side in all your dealings will also work wonders and infect everyone around you.

. . . in the Fourth House

The more outgoing and optimistic you are, the happier your home life will be. Not only will you feel better, but kith and kin will revel in your affectionate aura. A problem from the past may be resolved when you realize you've accepted it at last.

. . . in the Fifth House

A ravishing ring of confidence makes you stand out from the crowd now, so cash in on this propitious patch by using your unique talents and skills to the full. You're brimming with hope and happiness, so celebrate in style with your favourite folk!

. . . in the Sixth House

No matter how tedious the task, it'll be grist to your marvellous mill now for you're raring to go at work and clear the decks of anything outstanding. You're being carried along by your own momentum, and your sense of being on top of the world.

. . . in the Seventh House

You're top of everyone's pops now, but that's hardly surprising considering your sunny outlook and infectious high spirits. Relationships will be rosy, you'll grow even closer to a special someone and if you're solo you could soon attract an amour.

. . . in the Eighth House

Belief in your own abilities and confidence in your cause will open all sorts of financial doors that would otherwise remain firmly shut. If you've been wanting to make a fresh start with your other half then get talking now!

. . . in the Ninth House

Think big! That's the way to attract opportunity to your side now, so be as optimistic as you can and grab every chance that comes your way. If you're off on a trip then your enthusiasm and excitement will ensure it's a success. Enjoy yourself!

. . . in the Tenth House

When it comes to prestigious or professional prospects you've got every reason to be optimistic and hopeful now, for it's your positive attitude that will get results. Don't let anyone cast a damper over you, 'cos the stakes are too high!

. . . in the Eleventh House

Be yourself and friends will flock to your side! In fact, the more cheerful and outgoing you are, the better your life will be, especially where social settings or future plans are concerned. Plan ahead now and your enthusiasm will win the day.

. . . in the Twelfth House

Emotionally, you're riding high at the moment, so enjoy it whilst it lasts. Positive thinking brings positive results, and you're about to discover how true that is. Make the most of your increased insight and intuition and they'll pay dividends.

18 Moon

Divinatory meaning

Although very beautiful, the Moon can be highly deceptive for things look strange and different in moonlight – and confusion, illusion and delusion are the bywords of this card. Astrology links the Moon with our feelings and instincts, and so this card also signifies powerful and highly-charged emotions.

You may well feel as though you're trying to pick your way through a minefield of mistakes, muddles and misunderstandings. Nothing is quite as it seems at the moment, and that goes for the people you meet as well as the circumstances you find yourself in. Be especially wary of women now, for they could be up to no good or full of intense feelings that need an outlet.

Maybe you have to deal with a clinging mother who won't let her children sever the apron strings, a mendacious maiden who can't tell fact from fiction or a destructive damsel who's determined to trip you up?

You may also be unsure of a sweetheart's intentions, but whatever's wrong, your best bet is to trust in your instincts and intuition now for they'll help you detect friend from foe.

Creatively, you'll be truly inspired so make the most of your gifted imagination now.

Reversed meaning

Muddles and mix-ups are still in the offing when this confusing card is reversed, but they may not be as serious or upsetting as when the Moon is upright. You might also be afflicted with doubt or despair about your abilities to cope, and be in dire need of a sympathetic shoulder to cry on.

You could also be plagued by bad dreams, bouts of moodiness or a strange sense of impending doom that you just can't shake off. Women may suffer from menstrual or gynaecological problems when this card appears.

. . . in the First House

Follow your instincts and you won't go far wrong. That's the best way to tread a path through the minefield of deceit, disruption and dishonesty surrounding you now. The women you know will exert a powerful influence, but is it for good or ill?

. . . in the Second House

Think twice before parting with the pounds and pence, for what seems a smashing bargain or irresistible temptation in the shop may lose its attractions once you've got it home. Someone could also try to sell you a pig in a poke, so watch out.

. . . in the Third House

Don't believe everything you see or hear, for a close relative or neighbour may be playing tricks, or perhaps you've deliberately misunderstood? There's more than a hint of deception in the air, but if you follow your hunches all will be well.

. . . in the Fourth House

Delay making any important decisions on the domestic front, for matters may not be as simple as they seem. Listen to your strong intuition if in doubt! Women play a big role in your world now, but beware of one who's too tenacious by half.

. . . in the Fifth House

Loving liaisons could be a cause for current concern, so don't be surprised if a sweetheart thinks they own you or a child acts up, or perhaps you're playing games with someone's heart strings? A social rendezvous could be spoilt by a slip-up.

. . . in the Sixth House

If you're working round the clock or saddled with extra chores, then check you aren't slaving away whilst other folk have their feet up. You might be doing their job as well as your own so let your gut feelings be your guide. Sort out health worries too.

. . . in the Seventh House

Disillusionment or disappointment mar one-to-one affairs now, but instead of harbouring a grudge you must get those frustrated feelings out into the open. Clear the air before misunderstandings turn into something more damaging or dangerous.

. . . in the Eighth House

Let your hunches and piercing perceptions keep you on the straight and narrow now, especially if you suspect someone of chicanery. You're brimming with intense emotions but take care they don't turn into possessive or obsessive machinations.

. . . in the Ninth House

If you're planning a trip then be sure of the facts first, for things may not be as straightforward as they seem. If you've been led up the garden path lately then be philosophical, learn from your mistakes and trust your hunches in the future.

. . . in the Tenth House

With so much double-dealing and deceit surrounding career concerns and big business, rely on your intuition to sort out the sharks from the saints. A parent or older person could be using emotional blackmail to make you do their bidding.

. . . in the Eleventh House

Beware of a false or fairweather friend, or an acquaintance with Machiavellian motives. A dishonest damsel may be running rings round you too. Ensure you're honest even if no one else is, and make your intuition your best pal now.

. . . in the Twelfth House

Tuning into your instincts and intuition is your best policy. Stick to your guns even if they do seem to fly in the face of common sense for you're surrounded by mists of mischief or even malevolence in which nothing and no one is quite as they seem.

19 Sun

Divinatory meaning

This is a marvellous card, for it foretells happiness, contentment and satisfaction. In the illustration on the card, The Sun is radiating benevolence, goodness and warmth, and that's just what you can expect now!

Success will come to whichever area of the spread this card appears in, and be accompanied by energy, vigour and a ravishing ring of confidence. Workaday matters will go from strength to strength and you'll attract plenty of favourable attention from colleagues and superiors, whilst love affairs will be wonderful when they're blessed by the presence of The Sun. If you've been feeling under the weather, or worse, then you'll soon be on the road to recovery.

This card can also signify happy dealings with children, whether you're about to have a baby yourself, already have a young family or will just enjoy being with other people's children.

Reversed meaning

The boundless energy and happiness of the Sun is hard to repress, even when it's reversed, but some sort of delay, difficulty or disappointment may have to be overcome first. Perhaps your expectations are too unrealistic, or you feel a sense of anti-climax at the end of a project? Instead of feeling fed up, frustrated or discouraged, you'd do better to tailor your ambitions and hopes to fit the current circumstances.

If a love affair or long-term relationship isn't as happy as it might be then cracks could start to show now. Misplaced pride, conceit or arrogance could also cause trouble. There may be problems with children, too. Perhaps a child stirs up trouble, makes a nuisance of him or herself, or will soon fall ill?

. . . in the First House

Magnificent! Your current high spirits, sincerity and sheer *joie de vivre* make you stand out from the crowd and attract plenty of admiring glances. It's a smashing time for getting projects off the ground or impressing people with your super personality.

. . . in the Second House

You're sitting on top of the world, so celebrate by splashing out on some of life's luxuries. Enjoy your good mood whilst it lasts but don't invite trouble by spending more than you can afford. You may be very generous towards a loved one.

. . . in the Third House

When it comes to communications you're a real live wire now, emanating enthusiasm, energy and the confidence to command everyone's attention. You'll shine in social settings and community concerns will benefit from your sunny outlook.

. . . in the Fourth House

Home sweet home! Being with kith and kin will warm the cockles of your heart, for happiness and contentment can be found within your own four walls or the bosom of your family now. Any property deals, DIY or family pow-wows should go well.

. . . in the Fifth House

Love, enjoyment and entertainment are yours for the asking, so seek out social settings, surround yourself with the VIPs of your heart and revel in being the centre of attention. Creative, artistic or athletic activities will be ace.

. . . in the Sixth House

Your talent for organization's second to none now, and bound to catch the admiring eye of bosses, colleagues and clients. What's more, your easy-going attitude will brighten up the dullest job and get you through chores at twice your usual speed.

. . . in the Seventh House

Pleasure and partnerships of all persuasions go hand in hand now, and if you're half of a happy couple then you'll really be a devoted duo! If you've yet to tie the knot or find the one for you then wedding bells could ring out very very soon. . .

. . . in the Eighth House

There'll be no stopping you at the moment, for all your intimate affairs are positive, productive and personable. Sexually speaking you'll be like the last of the red-hot lovers, whilst joint money matters will prosper under your inspired guidance.

. . . in the Ninth House

Fancy a trip abroad? Whether it's a last-minute or a long-awaited jaunt, you'll have a terrific time and make some new pals along the way. Whatever you do, your philosophical approach to life will ensure happiness. A most satisfying time indeed.

. . . in the Tenth House

Professional or prestigious prospects couldn't be better, especially if you grab opportunties as they arise and let your aptitude and acumen shine out. Those goals and objectives are within your grasp, and you'll deserve all the success you get!

. . . in the Eleventh House

Your sunny disposition and altruistic attitude puts you at the top of everyone's hit parade now, so mix and mingle with your friends. It's also a super chance to increase your social circle by joining new clubs or societies. What an enjoyable interlude!

. . . in the Twelfth House

Sincerity, good feelings and love are all around you, flooding you with happiness and joy. Even if you've been plagued by worries lately they'll melt away now, leaving you at peace with the world. A romantic reverie will be the icing on your cake.

20 Judgement

Divinatory meaning

The illustration on this card shows a typical image of the day of judgement, with an angel (believed by some to be Gabriel) summoning men from their graves so they can atone for their sins. The main message of this card is that you should assess the past, consider your faults and be aware of your own actions in case they are harming other people or yourself. The image of the resurrection means you are being given another chance.

This card shows that you've reached the end of a chapter in your life, which can be anything from a relationship, job, enterprise or holiday to an unpleasant experience or sad situation. Before you embark on something new, you should look back over what has happened and think it through, with the satisfaction of knowing that you did your very best and can feel proud of yourself. Even though you may have struggled or suffered at the time, you'll feel now that you acted for the best or will be able to view the past in a positive and productive light.

This card can also have a more literal meaning, saying that a legal matter will turn out well and that justice will triumph. It can also appear when a divorce is on the way.

Reversed meaning

You will still have reached the end of a phase in your life when this card is reversed, but sadly when you come to review it you'll be left with a bitter taste in your mouth. Maybe you'll believe (rightly or wrongly) that you let yourself down, should have done more to help someone else or that you just didn't pull your weight when it was expected of you? However, indulging in endless remorse and recriminations won't put matters right, so work out why you acted in the way you did (be honest with yourself!) and then try to learn from your experiences so you won't make the same mistakes in the future. If you've been unkind or unfair to other people then they may get their own back now. Be warned that a legal matter may not go the way you want it. In a karmic or spiritual sense you are now held to account or are answerable for your past actions.

. . . in the First House

Dwell on the universal law of cause and effect before you make any major moves at the moment, for the actions you take will have a profound impact on the folk around you. Careful consideration now could spare hours of anguish later!

. . . in the Second House

The hour of reckoning has arrived in all affluent affairs, and if your outgoings have dwarfed your income then it's time to own up. Instead of wallowing in guilt, you've got to revise your pecuniary policy and plan for a firmer financial future.

. . . in the Third House

Are you a bit of a gossip or scandal-monger? Then don't be surprised if you're treated to a dose of your own medicine now and don't like it one bit! Clear your desk of any outstanding paperwork before folk have a good excuse to moan at you.

. . . in the Fourth House

If you're planning a house move or big changes to your abode then make sure you consult kith and kin before swinging into action. It's time to let bygones be bygones, so try to come to terms with any parts of your past that still cause you pain.

. . . in the Fifth House

The more honest you are with yourself, the better you'll fare, especially when it comes to decisions or dealings that affect your nearest and dearest. If you've always hidden your creative light under a bushel, then at last you'll see it shine out.

. . . in the Sixth House

If you've made any bloomers or howlers at work or in your daily doings then this is when they'll come to light. On the other hand, if you've been slaving away with nowt to show for it, at last you'll receive the recognition you deserve. Well done!

. . . in the Seventh House

The time has come to pour oil on any troubled waters in your relationships, especially if the rift or ruction shows no sign of abating otherwise. Remember, to err is human, to forgive divine. Speaking your mind will improve matters no end.

. . . in the Eighth House

You need to set your sights on the future, but first you must deal with the past. Instead of dreaming up a terrible revenge for any associates who've done you down, you should forgive and forget. Make sure all official dealings are in apple pie order.

. . . in the Ninth House

Mulling over the past will bring rich rewards now, for you'll learn from your experiences and grow emotionally and spiritually. It may even introduce you to a creed, code or concept that leads to the birth of a brand new you!

. . . in the Tenth House

A shining new future beckons, so step into it with a new-found confidence and capability! Instead of holding back or expecting failure, you must have faith in your talents and abilities and then march straight towards your goals.

. . . in the Eleventh House

Past acts of kindness or generosity will be repaid now in wonderful ways, but don't forget friends who've done you favours too. Someone could judge you on the company you keep, but only you know whether their fears are unfounded or not.

. . . in the Twelfth House

Carrying around a big burden of remorse or regret is just making you miserable, so stop worrying about things you can no longer control and put them behind you once and for all. The future is too promising to be ruined by guilt. Learn to live again!

21 *World*

Divinatory meaning

'The world is your oyster' is the main message of this card, which is the final card of the Major Arcana and therefore signifies the completion of all the lessons you have learned from the previous 21 cards. It is the right way up when the Sun is at the top of the card and symbolizes total fulfilment and spiritual enlightenment.

Everything comes to he who waits, and you're about to receive the rewards and recompenses you so richly deserve! If you've been working full steam ahead at a project, prototype or plan, this is when all your hard graft will come to fabulous fruition. Folk will also show their appreciation and admiration for all your efforts, and if you're trying to clamber up the ladder of success you'll attract the attention of VIPs and people in power who are happy to place their trust in you and help you on your way. Even if events seem to be conspiring against you at the moment, everything will work out for the best, so take heart!

This is a very favourable card, signifying complete fulfilment, but its importance is increased when surrounded by other positive cards.

Reversed meaning

Unlike so many other cards in this pack, The World is a most fortunate card even when reversed. Success is still yours for the taking, but there will be a small delay before you begin to enjoy the acclaim, applause and appreciation that are due to you. If you find yourself going over the same ground time and time again or are stuck in a wee rut, then have the courage to break free. So, don't be disheartened or diverted from working towards your goals and objectives, and keep thinking positive – good times are just around the corner, and everything comes to him or her who waits.

. . . in the First House

As you sow, so shall you reap! You'll receive from others whatever you give out now, and whether that's good or bad is up to you. Why not make the most of your current energy and charisma to win folks over and make success the name of your game?

. . . in the Second House

Watch your spending! You're in the mood for a shopping spree, but can you afford it? Beware of bargains that are really pigs in pokes, 'cos you'll get what you pay for now. You'll also be paid what you're worth.

. . . in the Third House

The harder you work the better the results will be, especially where studying is concerned. Concentrating on a particular subject will be better than flitting from one topic to another. Any activities associated with writing will be ace.

. . . in the Fourth House

Show a little tender loving care towards your kith and kin and they'll pay you back in kind. Past efforts will begin to pay off now, especially at home. Take care when buying or selling anything connected with your abode.

. . . in the Fifth House

Social settings will be ultra enjoyable and you'll be eager to take the lead, but don't hog all the limelight for folk will get their own back sooner or later. You're sure of what you want now but beware of being a bossyboots!

. . . in the Sixth House

Been sorting out routine details at home or work, or attending to tedious tasks? Well, all your hard work could lead to fantastic opportunities in the future, or even a complete change in the way you live your life!

. . . in the Seventh House

All one-to-one affairs are bloomin' wonderful now and blessed with balance and harmony, so make the most of them. An important new partnership is just around the corner, but you may have to take the initiative to get it moving.

. . . in the Eighth House

Your libido's certainly on the rise at the moment, making you passion personified, but take care not to be selfish or too self-centred. Sort out any outstanding tax affairs for a rebate could be on the cards.

. . . in the Ninth House

Travel broadens the mind and you could soon be given the chance to travel to pastures very new and different indeed. Make sure you cash in on this cosmopolitan sojourn as much as you can, but double-check all travel details before you depart.

. . . in the Tenth House

Golden opportunities beckon in all professional, prestigious and parental pursuits, and the harder you've worked in the past the better your rewards will be. The path to prosperity may even lead you in a new and exciting direction!

. . . in the Eleventh House

You're about to meet, mix and mingle with a new circle of chums in a different social setting. Grab every chance to get talking to interesting folk and you could make some firm new friends. Charitable or humanitarian work may also appeal.

. . . in the Twelfth House

Feeling fraught after some rigorous rides on life's emotional roller coaster? Then get far from the madding crowd or try some meditation or yoga. All those nagging worries will melt away, leaving you refreshed, rejuvenated and raring to go!

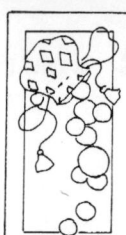

22 *Ace of Pentacles*

Divinatory meaning

The suit of pentacles (or coins) is the equivalent of diamonds in an ordinary pack of playing cards (diamonds decorate the bag in the illustration – this card is the right way up when this purse is at the top) and the astrological element of earth, and represents money (hence the bag of coins), status, material security and sensuality. The Ace of Pentacles is telling you to take the initiative in all materialistic and monetary matters, for this is a good opportunity to increase your coffers or strengthen your sense of security. Investigate ways of making your money grow now, whether you seek out safe but solid savings schemes, invest in possessions that will rise in value or sink your cash into an ambitious enterprise, business or partnership. Even if you start off with a wee nest-egg it will soon develop into a tidy little sum.

Hedonistic and sensual pleasures also mean a lot to you now, and you'll adore surrounding yourself with some of life's little luxuries, splashing out on a few treats or wining and dining your darling in stunning style. You'll also feel supremely sexy, making erotic encounters very enjoyable indeed and putting you at the peak of your passionate powers. No wonder Pentacles are linked with the astrological element of Earth!

Reversed meaning

Wanting a firm financial future is one thing, but beware of going overboard where acquisitiveness is concerned. Maybe you'll be reluctant to part with a penny more than you have to, want to get rich at others' expense or believe the world owes you a living? Whatever your motive, think twice before putting it into action for it could backfire.

Take care if a party or celebration is in the offing for it'll be easy to eat or drink too much, and sticking to a diet or health regime will be very hard going indeed! Your libido's also on the rise, but remember there's more to life than just sex.

. . . in the First House

Security, comfort and material well-being are what you're after! Your best policy is to use your personality to the full, for your sensuous charm and earthy aura will attract people to you and help you attain your goals.

. . . in the Second House

Any project, transaction or enterprise you're pursuing will not only be a success but will also increase your worth substantially. Concentrate on savings schemes or investment plans, and start building up a solid nest-egg for the future.

. . . in the Third House

Dealings and discussions about loot will go like clockwork and ensure a rosy future, but you'll lose, not gain, if you delay or let things slide. The post will bring you money or news of a financial fortune, for communications are connected with cash.

. . . in the Fourth House

Major investments associated with your abode bring long-term security now, making it a propitious time to sink your money into bricks and mortar. A woman may help you find a home at the right price, but its value will grow and grow.

. . . in the Fifth House

You're about to meet someone who'll shower you with gifts and goodies, despite being a wee bit boring. You'll make your own fortune now by cashing in on your talents and abilities, so don't let your current hedonistic mood make you lazy.

. . . in the Sixth House

Hard work and renewed effort will reap rich rewards in your working world whatever your professional status, ensuring a big bank balance for years to come. On the health front you should watch your diet and avoid overdoing the food and drink.

. . . in the Seventh House

A good relationship brings its own rewards now. Loyalty, trust and consideration will ensure happiness in a loving liaison, but professional partnerships will fare just as well if you help one another and complement each other's skills.

. . . in the Eighth House

You're in for a highly erotic and tactile time so cuddle up with your other half! Financially, you'll benefit from the generosity of others, and shared money matters will be prosperous. An inheritance or windfall is about to come your way.

. . . in the Ninth House

Cosmopolitan connections will help fill the coffers now, whether you leave these shores to find fame and fortune or work with someone from another land. A legal matter may be settled in your favour, bringing a financial bonus. Well done!

. . . in the Tenth House

You're heading straight for the top, and you'll be sure to hit the financial jackpot when you get there, even if you do have to wait a while before getting the power you crave. A golden handshake or monetary recompense could arrive via a career move.

. . . in the Eleventh House

A wealthy or worthwhile friend will give you tremendous backing, strong support or help you realize your many hopes and wishes. A hobby or pastime may provide some pin money or turn into a full-time occupation that's worth its weight in gold!

. . . in the Twelfth House

It may be hard to express your emotions now but you must be more demonstrative. If you're trying to make ends meet then help yourself by asking about charitable assistance, grants, benefits or supplements that will ease the boodle burden.

23 Ace of Wands

Divinatory meaning

The suit of wands (or rods or staves) from the Minor Arcana is the equivalent of clubs (shown twisting around the base of the torch) in ordinary playing cards and the astrological element of fire, and represents action, adventure, assertiveness and achievement.

The image of the burning torch on the card says you should seize the moment! Make the most of your current spirit of assertiveness, adventure and enterprise, for you're driven by powerful enthusiasm, energy and ambition now. In fact, it's definitely time to have a go at whatever you fancy, especially if it's something you've never tackled before. After all, you never know what you can do until you try, and you could really surprise yourself! Dynamic and exciting people, pastimes and places are all grist to your adventurous mill now, so don't stick to the true, tried and tested when you could strike out in new and different directions. The illustration on the card shows a flaming torch, and it's telling you to blaze a terrific trail through life. After all, the suit of Wands is linked to the astrological element of Fire!

Reversed meaning

Mind how you go, for you could easily get carried away by your own enthusiasm or momentum at the moment and end up poorer but wiser as a result. You'll still be fired with energy and enthusiasm, but instead of channelling them in the right directions you might fritter them away. Maybe you'll start lots of projects but fail to finish them, or spend so long making plans that there's no time to put them into practice?

Something else to watch is being so confident of your own abilities that you tackle tasks you know nothing about, or sell yourself so high that you'll never live up to everyone's expectations.

. . . in the First House

Be assertive, optimistic and enthusiastic, for that's the way to welcome success into your world. Gamble with life whilst your creative inspiration and confidence augur so well for the future. It's a time of new beginnings, initiatives and enterprises!

. . . in the Second House

Speculate to accumulate! Although you must curb impulsiveness and extravagance, you should still invest in anything that stands a good chance of coming up trumps. Cashing in on your own creative originality could bring home the boodle in abundance.

. . . in the Third House

Where you lead, others follow now! A neighbourhood or community concern will prosper with you at the helm, especially if you're fighting bureaucrats, autocrats or oppressive organizations. Good news will lead to an auspicious celebration.

. . . in the Fourth House

It's all change on the domestic front, for you're eager to transform your home life for the better. If you don't fancy moving then how about improving your present abode in some way? Glad tidings of a pregnancy or baby will spark off a shindig.

. . . in the Fifth House

This is one of the most prosperous and productive periods of your entire life! The germ of a creative idea will burst into being and bring untold success, an amorous alliance may be heaven on earth or a child or pet will make you glad to be alive.

. . . in the Sixth House

Make a fresh start in work and health matters, especially if you've been feeling below par or fed up. It will only take a spark of encouragement or reassurance to put you back on top of the world, so seek out the fresh opportunities around you.

. . . in the Seventh House

Close relationships are blessed with bliss, caring and sharing now, and if you're all alone then you'll meet a smashing sweetheart who knocks you off your pins. A wedding, anniversary or engagement party may mean new loving liaisons.

. . . in the Eighth House

Pungent passions pulsate through you but you'll only get intimately involved if amour is around. Even so, beware of starting an affair because you're bored or on the rebound. A joint money matter will do well if honesty is your watchword.

. . . in the Ninth House

It's time to broaden your horizons and expand beyond your usual boundaries, for a fresh and exciting cycle has started when almost anything's possible. The world's your oyster, so channel your unique talents in international directions!

. . . in the Tenth House

Beware of being arrogant, pompous or full of your own importance or you'll lose your current advantage. Your creative brilliance and dazzling personality will put rivals in the shade, ensuring applause, acclaim and prestige are yours for the taking.

. . . in the Eleventh House

You're on a voyage that will take you to the dizzy heights of fame and fortune! Anything you embark on will be destined for great things, just as long as you look at the small print and nitty gritty as well as the long-term prospects. Good luck!

. . . in the Twelfth House

Harness it in the right way and your magnificent intuition will help you get to the bottom of any emotional or subconscious problems that are troubling you. If you're dealing with a sticky situation then remember that least said, soonest mended. Shhh!

24 Ace of Swords

Divinatory meaning

The suit of swords from the Minor Arcana is related to spades in ordinary packs of playing cards (you can see them decorating the handle of the sword – this card is the right way up when the handle is at the top) and the astrological element of air, and represents our mental faculties, words and negotiations.

The shaft of light shining on the sword in the illustration represents intellectual activities, saying that the more you use your little grey cells the better you'll fare. Make the most of your logic, reasoning abilities and objective outlook, especially if you've got to do some trouble-shooting or problem-solving. Lateral thinking or forward plannning will also help you win through, so have faith in your mental mastery and don't be downhearted.

Negotations, discussions and debates will all see you shine, especially if you've got to outwit an opponent or make your mark with some red-hot ideas. You're a very impressive person to have around at the moment! Your powers of organization are also excellent now, for you're able to tell folk what to do or bring order out of chaos.

Reversed meaning

Anything from muddled thinking to delusions of grandeur are the unfortunate order of the day, for you've lost all sense of perspective and aren't viewing matters in their true light. Perhaps you're just not thinking things through or are acting in a thoughtless or unintelligent manner? On the other hand, you could be drunk on your own power and be behaving like a petty tyrant, throwing your weight around or acting like the great I am? What's worse is you may not even be aware of what you're doing, but you can bet other people will be taking note. Any legal or official dealings could also go awry, or you might be the victim of injustice or unfairness yourself.

. . . in the First House

You're entering a time of important personal change, so turn your back on past patterns of behaviour and actively look to the future. Using your charismatic personality will remove any obstacles on your path to progress. An enlightening time!

. . . in the Second House

Use your head and you'll make plenty of pecuniary progress, but wait for others to take the lead and you'll be left on the shelf. In fact, the more bright and clever you are, the better you'll fare. It's a grand time to sign contracts or put pen to paper.

. . . in the Third House

The more articulate, erudite and eloquent you are the more propitious your prospects, especially if you broadcast your ideas at meetings or interviews. Even so, you must be at your most disciplined and consistent to see things through to the end.

. . . in the Fourth House

Try to cultivate your finer feelings, especially towards a relative who's going through a bad patch. Encouragement, support and reassurance are needed by a woman in particular, but you may be unsympathetic, and lacking in compassion. What's wrong?

. . . in the Fifth House

Your ideal person must have the brains of Einstein and the looks of a Greek god or goddess, but does such a paragon exist? It's highly unlikely, but any affair will prosper through communication. Artistic ideas are worth their weight in gold.

. . . in the Sixth House

Keep calm! Nervous complaints or poor circulation will take their toll unless you can counter the stresses and strains of your working world. If your job won't let you take the initiative or think for yourself then it's time to find one that will.

. . . in the Seventh House

Your relationships will only prosper now if your partner has an active mind, for although you don't want a rival you do want someone who'll complement your own ideas. If that isn't possible then you must cultivate other bonds between you.

. . . in the Eighth House

Intimate affairs are disappointing and difficult now, so try to keep partnerships platonic whilst this chilly spell lasts, and beware of trading your physical favours for material needs. Joint agreements and affluent alliances will prosper, however.

. . . in the Ninth House

Knowledge is power, so consider acquiring extra qualifications, studying new subjects and generally enhancing your learning power. Travel's also good for you, for it'll teach you volumes about other countries, creeds and cultures.

. . . in the Tenth House

You'll reach the top on pure merit, thanks to your brainpower and abilities. You need a profession that will make full use of your education and intelligence, so why settle for less? A serious chat with a boss or father figure will go well.

. . . in the Eleventh House

It's time to launch long-term plans and promote your ideas, so don't delay! You'll do best if you work with others in a group, team or organization. An army of acquaintances surrounds you, but try to cultivate a true-blue friend too.

. . . in the Twelfth House

Despite being highly perceptive and intuitive, it's hard for you to express your emotions, perhaps because you like to seem rational and controlled? Well, showing your feelings will win you far more friends! A secret organization intrigues you.

25 Ace of Cups

Divinatory meaning

If you look at this card you'll see a ring of hearts around the rim of the brimming cup, and that's your clue to its meaning of emotional matters. The suit of cups from the Minor Arcana is the equivalent of the hearts in ordinary playing cards, and the element of water in astrology, and is closely associated with our emotions (symbolized by the hearts) and our unconscious (symbolized by the water).

The Ace of Cups is linked to emotional fulfilment, happiness, love and affection in all their fabulous forms. It can represent artistic talent, spiritual sensitivity and deep experiences, and may even foretell a new love affair, marriage or the birth of a baby if supported by other favourable cards. In fact, this is a wonderful card to appear in a spread, for a cascade of contentment, peace, harmony, amour and inspiration won't be far behind!

This card also signifies the ability to tune into other people's deepest feelings, and the knowledge that there are more important things in life than material objects.

Reversed meaning

Matters aren't nearly so rosy when this card is reversed, for then you can expect the opposite of all the good things described above. A love affair could come to an unhappy end, a relationship may hit the rocks, a partnership might go through a painful patch or you might be subjected to a tear-soaked string of disappointments and delays where loving liaisons are concerned.

You may also feel despondent, depressed, melancholy and miserable for no apparent reason, or be the victim of a close companion's confidence trick. Whatever happens now, don't let it make you bitter, resentful or determined to get your own back. Instead, remember the good times and believe that it really is better to have loved and lost than never to have loved at all.

. . . in the First House

You're more sensitive than at any other time, so are easily hurt and very vulnerable, particularly when it comes to your emotions. Watch your feelings, for although they could run away with you, they'll also imbue you with superb artistic inspiration.

. . . in the Second House

Financial improvement is on the cards, but only if you use your perfect artistic appreciation. Investing in things of beauty will be a sound monetary move. The sustenance, succour and support of others will be very welcome indeed if you're in a sorry state.

. . . in the Third House

You're a sucker for a hard luck story now, and close relatives or neighbours will be the ones crying the loudest. You'll gladly give your sympathy but don't take on their troubles too. Write to, phone or call on folk who can give you help or advice.

. . . in the Fourth House

You're not an emotional reservoir but your family seem to disagree, draining you dry emotionally and abusing your good nature. Maybe it's time to cut the apron strings? Fond memories will flood back or you may meet someone from the good old days.

. . . in the Fifth House

Creative ventures and enterprises find you at your most inspired, so put your unique talents to the test. Your love life will be tender and true, and there's more than a whiff of procreation in the air, whether you give birth to a babe or an artistic idea.

. . . in the Sixth House

Working in a selfless way to help others will bring you the greatest emotional fulfilment and satisfaction now. Look after your health, especially if you're prone to hypochondria or psychosomatic ailments, and get to the root of any problem.

. . . in the Seventh House

You want to transcend all your relationship worries, but if you do all the giving and your partner does all the taking then it's time to make some changes. Great joy and happiness are possible, but only if your amorous alliance is strong and satisfying.

. . . in the Eighth House

Steamy, sensual and erotic sums up the current state of your sexual desires, but if you're looking for true love too then you could be disappointed. Maybe you should lower your sights? Sadness or someone's sympathy may bring you a financial benefit.

. . . in the Ninth House

Being near water will bring you peace of mind now. You're also inspired mentally, so direct your energies towards the fine arts or classical literature and make the most of your civilized refinement. Spiritual philosophies and beliefs mean a lot too.

. . . in the Tenth House

Put your ego on the back burner and act with sensitivity and you'll achieve your ambitions, but assert yourself at the expense of others and you'll soon be sorry. A paternal link, whether emotional or spiritual, will be very strong now.

. . . in the Eleventh House

Everything you plan now should be for the good of others, or you won't make any progress at all. Someone you meet socially, or through an artistic group or society, will be kind, considerate and have an important effect on your destiny.

. . . in the Twelfth House

Strong feelings flood through you but don't get too sensitive or you'll suffer from an emotional backlash. Psychically you're second to none, so tune into your instincts and explore yoga, meditation or anything else that will act as enlightenment.

26 Aries

Divinatory meaning

There are three sorts of Arians – the randy ram who's a bossy egoist, the bouncy baa lamb who's a wee bit innocent and the silly sheep who follows others. They're all shown on the card with Little Bo Beep, but which one will you be? Aries is the first sign of the zodiac and associated with assertiveness, action and adventure.

The card is telling you to adopt a more dynamic and bolder approach to life, for taking a back seat or being a shrinking violet isn't the answer now. Seize the initiative and make the first move whenever possible, whether personally or professionally, otherwise important openings could pass you by.

If you usually put other folk's needs before your own then you should act out of character and be a wee bit selfish for a change. It's also a good time to be frank, forthright and completely honest, so speak your mind and don't beat about the bush. Your current ring of confidence should give you a helping hand!

Emotionally, you're lusty, lecherous and eager to put your fiery feelings into ardent actions, or maybe you're going to meet an Arian who acts like this and makes a big impression on you?

Reversed meaning

Keep calm and stop losing your temper! You're liable to let off steam at the drop of a hat, but try not to rant and rave at everyone who annoys you or you'll just build up trouble for yourself.

Another possible problem is being too competitive, for instead of pipping everyone else to the post you'll just tread on their toes and put their backs up.

Take care in emotional matters too, for you might come on so strong you make your amour think you're only after one thing. Alternatively, you'll come into contact with someone who shows the worst Arian traits.

. . . in the First House

Your current assertive and aggressive attitude will cause problems with loved ones if you ride roughshod over their needs and wishes. When it comes to personal ambitions though, you're really going places! All shades of red are lucky now.

. . . in the Second House

Earning money comes easy now, but it's your brawn that'll bring in the boodle, especially if your job's connected with martial, masculine or athletic activities. Beware of impulsive spending though! A man linked with loot will be important to you.

. . . in the Third House

You're communicating with great verve, vivacity and veracity, which will serve you well when standing up for your rights. Now's the time to write stiff letters or make tricky calls. Folk who threaten your neighbourhood will get short shrift from you.

. . . in the Fourth House

Someone's selfishness is stirring up trouble at home, turning it into a hot bed of arguments. You may be upset by the threat to your security, but don't only think of yourself. Try to control tempers and solve disputes before they get out of hand.

. . . in the Fifth House

Now's your chance to dash forward with any enterprise or idea that's entirely of your own making. Sporting activities will also see you shine. Loving liaisons are full of zest and zeal, for you exude a stunning amorous energy. Beware of a boisterous child.

. . . in the Sixth House

If you're self-employed then you're about to see speedy results and a rapid rise in your productivity. Whatever your daily doings, act with strength, industry and energy to carve a niche in your employment world or boss's eyes.

. . . in the Seventh House

Sharing things won't come easy now, so don't be surprised if your selfishness provokes a fight with a partner. Try to consider their feelings too. You'll come up against an adversary, but at least their antagonism will show you where you stand.

. . . in the Eighth House

You're a raging inferno of passion and desires – grand if you're half of a close couple but frustrating if you're not. If that's so then channel your energies into constructive concerns or you'll lash out in a violent or vitriolic way.

. . . in the Ninth House

You've just got to get on your soapbox and tell folk how you feel! If you're the victim of an injustice or lies then seek sage advice before blowing your top. Swing into ardent and assertive action if your enviroment's under threat.

. . . in the Tenth House

It's great to be ambitious but don't be inconsiderate or rude too! Your fervent and fiery ego will help you to be forceful in your career, but beware of ruthless folk who think you're a threat. A male boss or bigwig will be a help or a hindrance.

. . . in the Eleventh House

Although you'll fit in with the rest of the team in all walks of life you have an urge to show off and steal the limelight, but can you keep up the pace? Your future success depends on your skills and techniques, so don't try to do everything at once.

. . . in the Twelfth House

A sense of mystery surrounds you now. If you don't like it then all will be revealed soon. If someone's plotting against you they'll quickly give the game away. A man in prison, hospital or other institution will need your help.

27 Taurus

Divinatory meaning

The earthy, practical and prosaic sign of Taurus is symbolized here by a rustic farmer's wife. The bull in the background is the animal associated with this sign, and the food in the woman's basket represents the security that Taureans need so badly.

If you aren't born under the sign of Taurus then you must act as though you are now, by being down-to-earth, matter-of-fact and very practical indeed.

You'll also enjoy being out in the fresh air as much as possible, for the verdant countryside and wide open spaces will do you the world of good. Tending a garden or growing your own food can also fill you with contentment. Now's a good time to increase your sense of security with material possessions, although you should beware of setting too much store by them.

If you usually flit from one subject to another then seeing something through from start to finish will come easier now with a bit of effort. Fidelity and loyalty are also important to you, imbuing partnerships with extra affection and meaning, and it's a super time for relaxing in luxury with the ones you love.

Reversed meaning

Does 'stubborn as a mule' ring any bells? Either you're standing your ground and not moving an inch or you know someone else who's being obstinate and obdurate. Another possible problem is possessiveness, with folk acting as though they own each other or trying to lay down the law. You don't really believe a dear one is your property, do you?

If you wage a losing battle with your weight at the best of times then be extra careful now, for you could easily pile on the pounds or succumb to some gloriously gluttonous grub with no trouble at all!

Although you're viewing the world from a very practical position, don't let that turn into narrow-mindedness or a complete lack of imagination.

. . . in the First House

Sensuous, tactile and voluptuous, you exude an earthy attraction and inner strength that makes you very popular indeed. You adore everything that's natural, and music, food and love will fill your soul with joy. All shades of blue are lucky.

. . . in the Second House

You're on the hunt for acquisitions, possessions and anything else that'll add to your material wealth. The more time spent looking for treasures, the better the bargains you'll find, especially if you're after anything beautiful.

. . . in the Third House

Throw yourself into social settings and you'll not only have fun but also come into contact with all sorts of influential folk. A letter, phone call or visitor will bring good news on the amorous or financial front. Everyone loves you now!

... in the Fourth House

It's time to turn your home into a palace, but you're only interested in buying furniture and fittings that are sumptuous, splendid and as comfy as can be. You won't fancy going far, for you'd rather laze about at home with your feet up.

... in the Fifth House

Leisure and pleasure are what you want at the moment, so surround yourself with luxury and loved ones. A child or pet will mean great happiness, and a creative venture could go from strength to strength and bring home the bacon too.

... in the Sixth House

If your throat or liver are your weak spots then guard them carefully now. Over-indulging in the food and drink could cause health problems galore, so mind how you go. Your artistic talents will be brought to the fore at work.

... in the Seventh House

Beware of letting your heart rule your head, for that could lead to possessiveness or huffiness and ruin a perfectly good relationship. You're surrounded by folk who absolutely adore you, so don't upset them by getting the wrong end of the stick.

... in the Eighth House

Your sex life's sizzling with earthy fun and frolics, so stand by for close encounters of the cupidic kind. Someone may make you an offer that leads to money, for all shared financial affairs are prosperous and profitable now.

... in the Ninth House

You may be quite set in your ways at the moment, but something's telling you to be more adventurous and enterprising instead. Take a chance on an international link and it could turn into a gold-mine, or maybe you'll fall for someone from abroad?

... in the Tenth House

Prosperity is all around you, for you're imbued with a charm and dependability that'll impress bosses, bureaucrats and bigwigs. Use your personality and good looks to the full and prepare for prominence or promotion.

... in the Eleventh House

Your future plans rely entirely on how much money you can raise or how much help your friends are prepared to give. You'll make headway if you stay faithful to your cause, but don't expect instant results. Socially, you're on top form.

... in the Twelfth House

An air of secrecy hangs in the air, and you don't like it one bit. Maybe someone's trying to deceive you or they're about to let you down with a bump over a money matter or romantic rendezvous? Don't be lulled into a false sense of security.

28 Gemini

Divinatory meaning

There are two people on this card (in fact, they're the nursery rhyme characters Jack and Jill) because Gemini is the sign of the Twins and signifies communications. It works on two levels – one is high-minded and philosophical and the other one is gossipy.

This card either signifies that you're about to meet a Gemini or that you should act in a more Geminian manner by increasing your communications and using your mind as much as possible. Even if you're usually tongue-tied it'll be easy now to put your feelings into words, making it a grand time to clear the air with others or launch any ideas on the waiting world.

Don't be surprised if you feel bored or stuck in a rut, for you may need more stimulation and excitement than your usual surroundings can offer. Why not get out and about on short trips or explore your neighbourhood? Folk will find you fun to be with too, for you'll be witty, quick and clever. You're ready for variety to spice up your life.

Reversed meaning

Watch your tongue, for you could easily say something sarcastic, cutting or even cruel without even realizing it now. Communications are to the fore, but that doesn't mean you should devote your days to gossiping, spreading rumours or exaggerating the facts out of all proportion, you know!

Concentrating on the job in hand could be difficult at times, for your mind will jump from one idea to another at the first hint of boredom. Maybe you should make a point of doing several things at once, otherwise you could have nothing to show for all your efforts.

. . . in the First House

Your current eloquence and articulate attributes put you in the top league of communicators, and with your stimulating personality it'll be easy to get your own way. Try not to start anything you won't finish. Yellows will boost your luck.

. . . in the Second House

Use your ready wit or silver tongue to earn a living and you'll make a packet. Financial or money transactions look good, but read the small print first and don't get mixed up with crooks or con men. It's a good time to buy a computer or typewriter.

. . . in the Third House

You're a real social butterfly and will take some folk by storm with your friendly and fun-loving ways, though others may see you as superficial or trite. Steer clear of gossip and don't believe all you hear. Someone may be a fair-weather friend.

. . . in the Fourth House

You could soon be moving house, for your home life looks very busy indeed with plenty of comings and goings. If you're planning a move then head for the city, not the country. A young member of the clan could impart some startling news.

. . . in the Fifth House

Finish what you begin now, and your brilliant mind will send you straight up the ladder of success. However, it's up to you to promote, publicize and advertise your enterprises, so don't keep mum. A clever child will need plenty of encouragement.

. . . in the Sixth House

If you've got problems with your nerves, respiratory system or hands then seek medical advice. Is your job giving you gyp? If so, then find one that makes the most of your clever brain and your health should soon improve no end.

. . . in the Seventh House

You'll be true to someone in your fashion now, which means you want to have your cake and eat it! Oppressive or possessive partnerships don't appeal, for you need a relationship that fires your mind, not your body.

. . . in the Eighth House

Sexual peccadilloes are calling, and you're in the mood for experimenting! If your other half won't play ball then maybe your sex life needs to be teased out of its rut? You may have to sign some official forms, but read the small print first.

. . . in the Ninth House

Rigid restrictions and routines will really get your goat, making you long to escape. How about a short trip away? Physical, mental or emotional chains must be broken before they break you, so grab the chance to learn, travel and experience life anew.

. . . in the Tenth House

Make the most of your current witty and clever charms and you'll certainly go far. You may be very ambitious now but at least you know what you want! Any career calling for a good communicator will bring rewards, so have a chat with the boss.

. . . in the Eleventh House

It's a grand time to join a club or group, for you want to get to know folk and meet new people. If you're making long-term plans then you could hit on a wonderful idea that will open the floodgates of success. A Gemini could interest you now.

. . . in the Twelfth House

Supernatural subjects such as magic or the occult really appeal, making you long to embark on your own voyage of discovery. Just make sure you aren't fooled by someone who's out to trick you. Be wary of your over-active imagination!

29 Cancer

Divinatory meaning

Cancer is the sign of the Crab (there is a crab caught in the little girl's net), and belongs to the element of water, which rules the emotions. It is also the sign of motherhood and maternal instincts, as shown by the illustration on this card. The sea and the Moon (the planetary ruler of Cancer) represent our shifting emotions and our unconscious.

A maternal, cosy and comforting atmosphere surrounds you now, whether you meet a caring Cancerian or adopt a more Cancerian approach yourself. If that's the case, then spending more time with your kith and kin will warm the cockles of your heart and fill you with a deep contentment. Even staying at home or doing lots of cooking can make you happy, so revel in the comforts of your own abode. Now's a fine time to redecorate your dwelling too, or perhaps even up sticks and move house, for negotiations and arrangements will go well at the moment.

Listen to your intuition for it should be spot on, especially when it concerns your family, but your increased sensitivity may also mean you take offence more easily than usual or see slights when they don't really exist.

If you're off on a jaunt then head for the seaside. You'll love it!

Reversed meaning

Someone's got the hump, but who is it? If it's you, then try not to take everything so personally or you'll spend all your time sulking in silence or fighting back the tears.

Your nearest and dearest mean the world to you now, but don't show your fond feelings in possessive or clinging ways unless you want to frighten them off.

Another pitfall to beware of is pretending a relationship is hunky dory when in your heart of hearts you know it's over. Holding on to the past will do you more harm than good, so face up to childhood traumas or bad habits and banish them for ever. Insecurity and worrying about nothing are indicative of the Cancer card reversed.

. . . in the First House

How kind and considerate can you get? You'll do anything for anyone now, but don't let your current sensitivity turn into a moodiness that takes offence at the slightest opportunity. Silvers, whites and other pearly shades are the ones for you.

. . . in the Second House

Material security is important to you now, for you judge your worldly stability by what you have and hold. You're in the mood for collecting things but know what you're buying first! A family heirloom or long-lost treasure will mean a lot.

. . . in the Third House

Don't be surprised if neighbours, close relatives or friends come to you with their problems, for they'll have noticed how caring and sympathetic you are. You'll enjoy getting involved with local fund-raising or charitable concerns.

. . . in the Fourth House

Deep down you know that a current emotional problem calls for drastic action, but your fear of letting a loved one go stops you from acting. Be brave and get everything out in the open! A problem with a parent or the past needs a logical approach.

. . . in the Fifth House

An old flame may reappear in your life not only to gladden your heart but also prove you haven't lost your amorous appeal. News of a pregnancy or baby will make you want to celebrate, and a family get-together would suit you down to the ground.

. . . in the Sixth House

If you suffer from stomach trouble or women's problems then stop soldiering on and seek help instead, otherwise you'll just be tearful, tetchy and tense. Any work in which you're protective or of service to others will catch the eye of people in power.

. . . in the Seventh House

You may want a loving liaison to last forever and a day, but trying to put your affair in cold storage or standing in the way of change will swiftly bring it to an end. Tap your rich vein of emotions and you'll live together happily ever after!

. . . in the Eighth House

Your emotions are at an all-time high, ensuring you'll shower loved ones and close companions with more love and affection than they've ever known before. Just be careful not to smother them with your intense and compulsive feelings.

. . . in the Ninth House

If you're miles away from your roots and loved ones then write, phone or pop on a plane, otherwise you'll just feel insecure and unloved. An overseas opportunity could lead to emigration, especially if it means joining family who live far away.

. . . in the Tenth House

Your quiet ambitions could take some folk by surprise now, but you're determined to be successful and carve out a prestigious niche for yourself. Parental approval or past experience may have a profound effect on you, but don't let that stand in your way.

. . . in the Eleventh House

One half of you wants to cling on to the past whilst the other longs to stride into the future, but you can't hang on to tradition if it's just going to stunt your progress. You may say goodbye to a friend, but better chums are in the offing.

. . . in the Twelfth House

Let your emotions run away with you and it'll lead to trouble! Someone could take you for a ride and make the most of your current gullible and plausible persona – don't let them do it! Follow your intuition for it's your finest defence now.

30 Leo

Divinatory meaning

Leo is the most regal of the 12 Sun signs, so the illustration on the card shows that merry soul, Old King Cole. Leo is the sign of the lion, and a lion is painted on his bowl. Old King Cole represents the warmth and generosity of Leo, and the throne signifies his justifiably high opinion of himself.

Personality plus! That's the only way to describe you at the moment, so make the most of this sociable patch by mixing and mingling with VIPs of your heart. Exploring your creative talents will also be rewarding, for your innate artistry is enhanced and expanded in a host of wonderful ways. Your confidence has also been given a big boost, especially if you're usually a wee bit shy and retiring. This is no time to hide your light under a bushel for instead it should shine forth in a blaze of glory! Loved ones will enjoy your company too, for all your warmth, generosity and affection is being brought to the surface. You're as merry as Old King Cole! Revel in this happy phase whilst it lasts and indulge yourself in love, leisure and pleasure.

Reversed meaning

Get off your high horse at once and stop strutting around in that pompous way! Being too self-centred and sure of your own importance is the danger now, or perhaps you'll have to deal with someone who thinks they're the centre of the universe? Either way, you should resist the temptation to be conceited, self-important or too opinionated for words. Digging in your heels and standing your ground is another possible problem, 'cos it's one thing to be dignified and quite another to be so dogmatic.

Something else to watch for is letting your organizational skills turn into a lust for power that overturns everything in its path. Arrogance and a Narcissus complex show in others, or could it be in you?

. . . in the First House

Your sunny disposition and sparkling personality give you a head start when it comes to anything that's important to you. Bring out your inner warmth, be yourself and you won't go wrong. Your lucky colours range from sunshine yellow to pure gold.

. . . in the Second House

That love of luxury will lead to all sorts of cash complications unless you're careful, so go easy on the spending. Quality means more to you than quantity, but even so you must live within your means. Something made from gold could become a lucky charm.

. . . in the Third House

You're acting very proud, and maybe arrogant too, but is that wise? Your organizational skills are ace, but don't swagger and strut around or folk will think you're bossy and bombastic. Be aware of your motives before you act.

. . . in the Fourth House

Kith and kin mean a lot to you now, for you want to protect them as much as possible. That's grand, but don't smother or molly-coddle them. A loving and luxurious home life is promised, making it a grand time to enhance your abode.

. . . in the Fifth House

Love's top priority now, for it makes you glad to be alive. Someone may enter your life and steal your heart, which you'll gladly surrender, or an existing affair will be renewed and revitalized. Children or creative projects bring you pleasure.

. . . in the Sixth House

If you're prone to heart, circulatory or spinal problems then take extra care of yourself now. On the work front you'll get on well with bosses, but not if that means taking orders from them – you want to be the one in charge now. Watch it!

. . . in the Seventh House

Rich affections and fond feelings are to the fore, turning all your partnerships into a panoply of pleasure. It's a smashing time to tell a sweetheart how wonderful they are, though you'll be impatient and upset if they don't return the compliment.

. . . in the Eighth House

A straightforward sexual encounter will leave you reeling, because an exotic and erotic interlude's just what you need to put you on top of the world. Got anyone in mind? You'll also benefit from the generosity of others now.

. . . in the Ninth House

Is your life in the doldrums? Then consider making a major move to another country or getting in touch with folk from other creeds or climes. All artistic activities attract you too, so head for an art gallery, theatre, cinema or other cultural place.

. . . in the Tenth House

You've got what it takes to be a success, but the trouble is you won't be content with second best. Instead, you want to steal the show, and why not? You're truly gifted when it comes to dealing with the public but don't be arrogant or put on airs.

. . . in the Eleventh House

Sign up with a group endeavour or joint activity and you'll advance your future plans so successfully you could end up an entrepreneur! You're acting in a flashy and showy way so add a little humility. A Leo lad or lass may enter your life.

. . . in the Twelfth House

It's a difficult and disturbing time, for you've got to hide your feelings and disguise your true self. That could make your health suffer when you get confused about what's really going on. Keep to yourself and don't wear your heart on your sleeve.

31 Virgo

Divinatory meaning

Traditionally, the sign of Virgo is represented by Ceres, and so here is Mary Mary Quite Contrary watering her garden which is characteristically very neat (Virgos are very orderly). Virgo is a sign associated with practicality, organization, ideas and being of service to others.

Practical and pragmatic are the words to remember at the moment, for this is your chance to show the world how organized and accurate you can be when you try – or maybe you meet someone who's a shining example of a methodical and meticulous Virgo?

Either way, it's a grand time to be of service to others, especially at work or in a medical matter, so if your job involves helping folk then it should go like clockwork now. Any activities associated with gardening will go well too, and do you a power of good into the bargain! Communications are also on the up, helping you to put your feelings into words, especially when it comes to describing your latest brainwave or scheme. You'll be clever with your hands, making it a grand time to make or mend anything fiddly or intricate. Gathering facts and information is your forte now.

Reversed meaning

Ouch! Someone's sharp speech, carping criticism or sarcastic tongue is about to cut you to the quick - or are you the one who's telling folk where they've gone wrong? If so, then try to resist the temptation to find fault with everything and everyone and work out what's really wrong. Perhaps you're suffering from a severe lack of confidence?

It's a good time to look after your health or embark on a new diet or exercise regime, but beware of going overboard and turning into a complete hypochondriac who thinks they've got every ailment under the sun!

Virgo's usually associated with tidiness, but that isn't the case at the moment. In fact, your home probably looks like a bomb's hit it!

. . . in the First House

Shy, modest, retiring and unpretentious – that's you at the moment. You'd rather work quietly on the side lines than be in the limelight, but take time to relax or your nerves will soon be frayed and fraught. All autumn and harvest shades are fortunate.

. . . in the Second House

It's time for a thorough review of your material world, from spending money to savings, so you can keep track of the pounds and pence. Go through statements, accounts, bills and invoices with a fine-tooth comb. If you need a loan then speak up now.

. . . in the Third House

You're chatty, chirpy and curious at the moment, but don't be too inquisitive or folk could think you're checking up on them. Beware of being too critical or analytical as well. It's a grand time to make lists, gather news and broadcast it to others!

. . . in the Fourth House

If the housework's a real chore then why not invest in some labour-saving gadgets and equipment? Being tidy and having everything in its place is imperative for a smoothly run home. Spick and span is your domestic motto now!

. . . in the Fifth House

All work and no play makes you dull, so pursue pleasure with as much verve, vitality and vigour as you can muster. A child could be too clever by half. If your love life's lethargic then dropping your prim and proper approach should do the trick!

. . . in the Sixth House

Your diligence, dedication and industry will impress everyone around you, so keep up the good work and you'll even surprise yourself. Health and hygiene are also important, especially if you've let things slide lately. Time for a big brush up!

. . . in the Seventh House

Commercial partnerships look great, making it an auspicious time to conclude deals or join forces with like-minded folk. Loving liaisons will just languish, though, unless you can express your emotions more and show your sweetheart your softer side.

. . . in the Eighth House

Emotionally, you're so clinical and precise you're likely to chase away any prospective partners, whether sexual or financial. Working out why you feel frigid and frosty will put you nearer to an intimate relationship or spice up your current one.

. . . in the Ninth House

Make the most of your intelligent and studious self and you can gain valuable qualifications and respect. An opportunity or message may come from overseas. Be adventurous, especially when travelling, for who knows what awaits you!

. . . in the Tenth House

Instead of being cross about the current state of your career, why not seek help from folk who can arouse your ambitions and encourage you into action? Find a profession that lets you use your head and communicate with others, and you'll go far.

. . . in the Eleventh House

It's a good idea to make long-term plans but don't get so bogged down in tiny details that you lose sight of the overall picture. Maybe a friend could act as a helpful sounding board? A Virgo may enter your life as a platonic pal.

. . . in the Twelfth House

Anyone seeking sympathy will get short shrift from you now, for you've no time for folk with sob stories or who feel sorry for themselves. Even so, try not to be too harsh, moralistic or judgemental – have you never made mistakes or been miserable?

32 Libra

Divinatory meaning

The Sun sign of Libra governs relationships and permanent partnerships. Librans are very diplomatic, love luxury, hate anything ugly and can't abide rows or difficult atmospheres. This is the sign of the Scales (representing the Libran need for harmony and balance), and scales decorate this fairy's skirt.

Anything for a quiet life! That's your motto of the moment, for you're only interested in people or places that are happy and harmonious. One-to-one affairs are at the forefront of your world now and you'll find it easier to get on with others than usual. It's a smashing time to join forces with like-minded folk, whether that means plighting your troth to your one true love or pairing up for a professional partnership. On the other hand, if you've fallen out with someone, now's your chance to make amends, talk out your differences and get things back on an even keel.

Treating yourself to some of the luxuries of life is a good idea, especially if you normally put others first and yourself second. Why not splash out on some super scent, blissful bath oil or aromatic aftershave? Not only will you increase your powers of attraction but you'll pamper yourself into the bargain!

Reversed meaning

Tread carefully in all alliances, for rifts could appear at a moment's notice and leave you wondering what went wrong. Maybe you've turned a blind eye to problems that were obvious to everyone else, or a so-called friend has been treating your partner to a few home truths behind your back? Either way, you may be forced to admit a relationship's reached the end of the road. There's no point in hanging on just because you're too frightened to let go. You've a tendency to try to please everyone when it's simply not possible.

Another problem is indecision, for making up your mind might be almost impossible at the moment. You're able to see both sides of every argument, which means you're torn between the devil and the deep blue sea. Go on, be decisive!

. . . in the First House

Your charm, grace and elegance will bowl folk over now, especially when combined with your courteous and diplomatic ways. In fact, your glittering personality will help to promote all personal plans. Baby blues and sugary pinks are the hues for you.

. . . in the Second House

You long to be surrounded by all things bright and beautiful, but don't splash out if you can't afford it, or fork out cash for trash. Remember, all that glisters is not gold. You'll make much more money by putting your personality to the fore!

. . . in the Third House

Convivial and congenial, you're in a class of your own when it comes to entertaining folk. Mixing with people will do you a great deal of good when you need some help and advice. You'll hear good or bad news of a wedding or partnership.

. . . in the Fourth House

If your home life's anything but happy this is your chance to do sommat about it. Repair any rifts with relatives, decorate your dwelling if it's drab or think about moving if you're unhappy in your current abode. You can make big changes now!

. . . in the Fifth House

Love is all around you now, so why not wallow in its heavenly radiance and soak up all the affection and attention surrounding you? If you're single, you could meet someone who sets your heart racing and your pulses pounding. Lovely!

. . . in the Sixth House

Work's a real bore right now, but do you know why? Maybe you're just not in the mood, but if the problem goes deeper than that then why not look for a new job that makes the most of your skills? Watch out for backache, kidney or bladder disorders.

. . . in the Seventh House

Relationships are all about give and take, but if you're the one who does all the giving, then stand up for yourself or cut your losses. Happy couples will go from strength to strength, and if you're single then you won't stay that way for long!

. . . in the Eighth House

Keeping an even keel in intimate affairs is vital, otherwise jealousy and envy will rear their ugly heads. The trouble is, one of you wants pure love whilst the other's interested in impure lust! Intense emotions could also cause chaos in cash concerns.

. . . in the Ninth House

Refinement and sophistication are what you want, and you might meet someone who embodies them both. International events are also intriguing, and you'll enjoy immersing yourself in the culture of other countries and civilizations.

. . . in the Tenth House

Any career that brings out your personality is perfect, for you've an even-tempered, amiable and affable approach that will put people at their ease and pour oil on any troubled waters. Your charm and tact are your greatest assets now.

. . . in the Eleventh House

You're supremely sociable, so arrange get-togethers, outings and parties with your favourite folk. You might even make some useful contacts that help you map out your route for the future. Two heads are better than one in long-term plans.

. . . in the Twelfth House

Romantic reveries and escapist fantasies appeal to you now, but beware of idealizing a sweetheart or situation too much or you could get hurt. Your imagination is fabulously fertile in anything associated with the arts, music or dance, so let it rip!

33 Scorpio

Divinatory meaning

Scorpio is the most secretive, mysterious and intense sign of all (which is why the figure is hiding behind a mask), and has three very different sides, all of which are shown on the card. The dove is the peace-loving Scorpio, the eagle is the dare-devil one and the snake is the sly Scorpio that's always up to no good.

Prepare to be overwhelmed by profound and powerful passions, whether they well up inside you or you're deluged by the deep emotions of a close companion. One thing's for sure, you shouldn't underestimate anyone now, for they could take you by surprise when you least expect it, especially where intimate or financial affairs are concerned.

If you're usually a bit of a blabbermouth then now's the time to take a leaf or two out of Scorpio's book and keep mum. Some things may be better left unsaid at the moment, or maybe you're entrusted with a secret that you can't reveal even though you want to?

On the other hand, you might have to deal with someone who plays their cards very close to their chest or who seems determined to keep you in the dark over an important issue. You're in for a most mysterious time!

Reversed meaning

Unpleasant undercurrents or underhand actions are on the agenda, so watch your step at all times. If you're the one who's indulging in Machiavellian machinations then proceed with extreme caution, for you could invite some very determined and desperate opposition. Alternatively, you may meet a man or maiden who's manipulative, mendacious or powered by misguided motives.

A sexual set-up might also suffer, when either you or your other half is caught in the grip of oppressive and obsessive passions that soon turn into jealousy or envy. Beware of playing psychological games with a possessive partner for you might stir up a hornet's nest. A shared monetary matter may also spark off some compulsive or coercive actions.

. . . in the First House

Enigmatic, mysterious and secretive sums you up now, and keeping someone guessing could pay off in some interesting ways. Your personal allure will leave folk bewitched, bothered and bewildered. Dramatic dark colours will bode well.

. . . in the Second House

Money is power for you at the moment, but tread carefully for there are criminals, con-men and other shady characters around who could set tricky traps for you. Avoid underhand financial deals or you'll lose out in the long run.

. . . in the Third House

If secret talks and discussions come to light they'll certainly put the cat amongst the pigeons, so keep a discreet distance from known gossips in case they blow your cover. Act swiftly over official letters or communications from folk in uniform.

. . . in the Fourth House

If you're unhappy at home then maybe it's because you haven't got the privacy you need? A pond or pool will also bring you homely harmony now. A family member may be meddling in someone else's affairs and heading for trouble, so be warned.

. . . in the Fifth House

Passion personified, that's you! You express your love with such atomic force and profound pleasure that dear ones will find it hard to resist you. A new amour may be just around the corner, but are you ready for the strength of their seething passion?

. . . in the Sixth House

If you're unhappy with your workaday world then make changes before fate does it for you. A power-mad boss may try to take advantage of you, but resist rising to the bait or fighting might with might. You could fall foul of a mystery malaise.

. . . in the Seventh House

One-to-one affairs leave much to be desired, with psychological battles and power struggles going on behind the scenes. If you're trying to gain control over someone then you'll end up with nowt, or maybe a close companion's playing games with you?

. . . in the Eighth House

There will soon be a re-birth in your life, but first you must let go of the old you and prepare for this radical transformation. You could get involved in a sexual relationship that exerts a compulsive hold, no matter what you do to avoid it.

. . . in the Ninth House

All things metaphysical or occult appeal to you now, and the more you study them the more enlightened you'll be. You may soon be invited on a mystery trip or travel to a country shrouded in secrecy. Someone's motives go deeper than you think.

. . . in the Tenth House

Power's what you want at the moment, and any folk who stand in your way will soon realize how ruthless you can be. If this doesn't sound like you, then you'll soon have to deal with someone who's out for all they can get. Don't provoke them.

. . . in the Eleventh House

A very powerful friend is about to help you, especially if you don't know which way to turn in a future plan. This pal will pull hefty strings on your behalf. A Scorpio could be hell-bent on capturing your attention, but is it for good or ill?

. . . in the Twelfth House

Follow your psychic feelings and flashes of instinct for they're spot on and could lead to untold successes and even help you to control your own destiny. However, you must know your own strengths and weaknesses, otherwise you'll simply self-destruct.

34 Sagittarius

Divinatory meaning

Sagittarius is the sign of the Archer, who symbolizes the Sagittarian need for challenge. Sagittarians brim with boundless enthusiasm and optimism, and are also keen travellers – as shown by the signpost at the top of the card and the prancing horse.

Aim high! That's what the cards are telling you to do now, so rise to every challenge, act the optimist at all times and don't take no for an answer. Make the most of your current adventurous attitude and approach to life, and you'll be amazed at what you can achieve! Foreign links and cosmopolitan concerns will also pay dividends, increasing your insight into the ways of the world, introducing you to some influential folk and being entertaining and enjoyable into the bargain. Grab every opportunity to go travelling far afield, whether for business or pleasure, or foster international relations at home by getting to know folk from other creeds, countries and cultures.

Studying spiritual or academic subjects will also appeal, or how about learning a new language or signing up for a further education course? It could lead to all sorts of exciting opportunities and openings. A more philosophical approach will help in any current life situations.

Reversed meaning

Don't believe all you hear at the moment, for someone's good at embroidering the plain truth into a tale that's much more exciting. Or are you the one who keeps exaggerating?

Sagittarius is a sign that's renowned for looking on the bright side, but there's a danger now of indulging in blind optimism that automatically assumes everything will work out in the end. On the other hand, you may have to deal with someone who's talking and acting in an unrealistic and foolhardy fashion.

You may be desperate to escape your usual surroundings now but be unable to do anything about it. A trip might have to be cancelled at the last minute, but try to get away from your routine even if it's just for a day.

. . . in the First House

Your infectious enthusiasm, good humour, high spirits and bonhomie make you a very popular person. Watch out for minor mishaps as you're more than a wee bit clumsy now. Don imperial reds and purples to make the most of Lady Luck.

. . . in the Second House

Impulsive spending's on the agenda, for you're eager to splash out on little luxuries for yourself. Wins and windfalls could come your way, and you'll consider making a major purchase, but make sure you've got the boodle before you commit yourself.

. . . in the Third House

Big talk and false promises won't endear you to others when you fail to deliver the goods, or maybe you're taken in by folk who are all hot air? A letter or call may bring good news of a far-off loved one. There could be contact with Australia.

. . . in the Fourth House

If your current abode is too small for your needs then it's time to think of moving to somewhere more suitable. Other domestic changes could also be on the cards, either with a new relative on the way or one of the clan about to emigrate or leave home.

. . . in the Fifth House

Enjoy yourself doing what comes naturally! You're happy to be the centre of attention now, especially by showing off your creative talents, but you'll be just as happy appreciating the artistic attributes of others. A little love could come your way!

. . . in the Sixth House

You want to aim for the stars, but your current job won't give you the option or the opportunities. Well, it's time to set up on your own or switch firms to one that offers what you want. Don't over-indulge the grub or grog, or you'll feel liverish and low.

. . . in the Seventh House

Freedom and independence are what you need from a relationship, so you'll long to escape if your partner's possessive or predatory. But if you give each other independence then your liaison will go from strength to strength.

. . . in the Eighth House

Good fortune will come your way thanks to the benevolence of others. Money could arrive through an insurance policy or inheritance just when you need it most. Someone who only has eyes for you will bring you plenty of sexual satisfaction.

. . . in the Ninth House

You can't abide your present limitations any longer, for you want to spread your wings and fly off into the wide blue yonder. Well, what's stopping you? You have the luck of the gods at the moment, and everything you do will be blessed with success.

. . . in the Tenth House

Star luck is shining on your career, and that means you're really going places. The more your profession allows you to explore and expand your talents, the better you'll fare. Beware of being arrogant though or you'll clash with folk further up the ladder.

. . . in the Eleventh House

Events that take place now will reveal who your true friends are and which ones are just the fair-weather kind. You could be surprised at what you discover. A Sagittarian will have a big influence on you and could give you some ideas about your future.

. . . in the Twelfth House

You may have to deal with someone who is restricted or handicapped in some way, but you must realize you can't take on their problems. Instead, seek expert help on their behalf. This is a very philosophical and spiritual time for you.

35 Capricorn

Divinatory meaning

Capricorn is the sign of the Goat (you can see a little goat at the bottom of the card) and, just like goats clambering up mountains, Capricorns are good at climbing to the very peak of success. That's why this card is illustrated with Jack and the Beanstalk, as Jack is steadfastly making his way to the top of the beanstalk in true Capricorn fashion.

The more diligent, dutiful and detailed you are the better now, so pluck a few leaves from the Capricorn book of behaviour and show superiors how responsible and reliable you can be. Duties and obligations are grist to your mill, but be careful not to get too bogged down in red tape or imagine you're indispensable! You must spare some time for enjoyment too! A very ambitious attitude will secure success.

If you've been slogging away for years trying to make a name for yourself or earn the praise of your peers, then this card suggests you're about to receive the rewards you so richly deserve. Professional or prestigious pursuits will put you in the limelight, bringing you the beginnings of the honour, status or prestige you've always wanted.

Reversed meaning

It's all too easy to be doomy, depressed and downright dreary at the moment, but make every effort you can to shake off that pessimistic approach to life and be positive instead.

You could feel full of guilt without knowing why, or maybe you're deluged by duties and onerous obligations that you just can't escape?

Dealings with parents, bigwigs or bosses could be on the difficult side, especially if they refuse to give you the credit you deserve. You may think you're banging your head against a brick wall right now where your ambitions or career are concerned, but if you persevere you'll win through in the end!

Take care not to come across as too stuffy or starchy.

. . . in the First House

Lift yourself out of the doldrums, then turn on your delicious sense of humour and show folk you're a little ray of sunshine underneath that cloudy exterior. Blacks and greys will show just how sophisticated you can be.

. . . in the Second House

Empire-build as much as you can now, for this is when you can lay the firm foundations for a fabulous financial future. Anything from property to other possessions that'll increase in value are good investments and will increase your sense of security.

. . . in the Third House

Conflict with a local authority is on the cards, especially if you're dealing with folk who aren't pulling their weight. A letter or phone call from an older relative will bring glad tidings, but someone else may give you disappointing news.

. . . in the Fourth House

If an older person or parent is getting on your nerves then maybe it's because you're clinging on to a childhood image of them or aren't being as tolerant as usual. Have a good look round your abode in case it's in dire need of structural repairs.

. . . in the Fifth House

The classic and more serious side of the arts will bring you hours of pleasure now, so soak yourself in anything from opera to ballet. Any enterprise or venture based on your own talents is destined for success, but don't expect immediate results.

. . . in the Sixth House

Your health needs special care and attention, especially if you're suffering from a chronic illness or any ailment that curbs your mobility. If a job ends then see it as a new start to your life, or change your current work to something you really enjoy.

. . . in the Seventh House

The longer your relationship has lasted the greater its chances of success and happiness. If it's just begun then prepare for some rough patches ahead, though any age gap between you will help, not hinder. Business alliances will prosper.

. . . in the Eighth House

A sense of mystery or something macabre surrounds you now, or you'll become fascinated by the supernatural or occult. It's a fine financial time to investigate insurances or endowments, or to pool your resources with like-minded folk.

. . . in the Ninth House

Studious and academic, you're in pursuit of excellence and want to educate yourself above your social standing. What are you waiting for? A business offer may come from overseas or perhaps you're given the chance to travel.

. . . in the Tenth House

Your aims and ambitions are stronger than ever before, for you really want to achieve something in this life. Well, now's the time to start, for sheer determination and hard work will put you where you want to be. Honour and prestige await you.

. . . in the Eleventh House

A pensioner, parent or older pal will get involved in your long-term plans, so listen to their advice before making up your own mind. The actions you take now will help to build the foundations for your future success, so act wisely and well.

. . . in the Twelfth House

You're feeling emotionally imprisoned and isolated, but wallowing in misery will only make matters worse. Instead, learn from past experience then put your mistakes behind you and start to rebuild your life. Things aren't as bad as you think.

36 Aquarius

Divinatory meaning

Aquarians are way ahead of their time, as shown on the card by the figure shooting off to the stars on a space ship. They are the most idiosyncratic members of the zodiac and the rainbow represents the many facets of their dazzling personalities. The bucket of water is a reminder of their symbol of the Water Carrier.

Dare to be different! That's the message to remember, for this is your chance to stand out from the crowd and show everyone what a unique and original person you really are. Even if you usually hide behind tradition and a conservative outlook, it's time to break free from the ties that bind you and bring out the more unconventional and unusual you. Anything or anyone that seems predictable, pedantic or pompous will make you mad, 'cos you've got no time for folk who are stuck in a rut or who abide by rigid routines.

Some people may think you're being too avant-garde and outrageous at the moment, but have the confidence of your convictions and stick to your guns, for you're way ahead of your time and will leave others standing as you blaze a terrific trail. There's no stopping you now, for the more exclusive, unique and individual you are the better.

Reversed meaning

A mixed bag of fortunes awaits you. You may meet a quirky Aquarian whose oddball antics leave you reeling with shock and surprise. On the other hand, you might be overcome by bizarre behaviour that veers between brilliance and being bonkers. If so, then try to be aware of what you're doing, and beware of upsetting too many people with your *risqué* or rebellious ways.

If you're raring to go on plans and projects for the future, then you could come into contact with a right old stick-in-the-mud who seems determined to block your every move. Someone's intransigence, intractability or wilful ways could also upset the apple cart, or leave your nerves frayed and frazzled. Take care!

. . . in the First House

Your charisma and personal magnetism electrifies everyone you meet now as you cast a magical spell over them and prove what a star you are. This is your chance to push your interests forward. Electric blues will show you at your best.

. . . in the Second House

The more unusual your job or source of income, the more money you'll make at the moment. It's a good time to buy hi-tech gadgets like faxes or computers, or to invest your loot in anything that's a wee bit out of the ordinary.

. . . in the Third House

Taking a fresh approach to an old problem will work wonders, and you'll also make an impact on others by being a little radical and controversial. A shock or surprise from a sibling or neighbour will call for quick thinking on your part.

. . . in the Fourth House

What you need now is an abode that's different and exciting, so look at designs, decorations or devices that set it apart from the others in your street. An unusual family circumstance will take you by surprise, or a relative could act out of character.

. . . in the Fifth House

You may hear unexpected or unbelievable news about a child or pet now. A short-lived amorous affair could leave you titillated, or maybe you fall for a friend? Your inventive skills and creative abilities will combine to bring you success.

. . . in the Sixth House

Taking orders from others is impossible now, for you want to be boss. Any job with modern or scientific overtones will do well, although you'll succeed in any career that's different or unusual. Try to relax or you'll end up tense and troubled.

. . . in the Seventh House

The more permissive and liberated your relationship, the happier you'll be now, but if you're naturally jealous and possessive then you're asking for trouble. Avoid issuing ultimatums, demands or threats to partners, because if you do you'll lose the lot.

. . . in the Eighth House

Those unpredictable emotions of yours will put everyone on edge, especially in your intimate affairs. Why not own up to your sexual fantasies and desires instead of hiding them? Unforeseen circumstances may bring a wee windfall your way.

. . . in the Ninth House

Unorthodox and unconventional topics attract you, so delve deep into anything from astrology to alternative religions. Folk who are narrow-minded or bigoted will get short shrift from you. A journey to an out-of-the-way place will be exciting.

. . . in the Tenth House

Taking orders or having to toe the line is anathema to you at the moment, so the more scope your career offers you the happier you'll be. Whatever the path you're treading through life, a sudden change of direction is on the cards.

. . . in the Eleventh House

Friendships and fidelity are of vital importance, and a pal may occupy as big a place in your heart as your closest family. The folk you meet now will be excitingly different. Long-term plans may face opposition before they finally succeed.

. . . in the Twelfth House

Follow your intuition and perception and you won't go far wrong. Metaphysical or supernatural subjects will enthral you, whilst opening up parts of your personality you never knew existed. Enjoy discovering the hidden side of yourself!

37 Pisces

Divinatory meaning

Pisces is the most mystical and fantasial sign of all, so is represented here by that mythical creature, the mermaid. Pisces is the sign of the Fish, which are shown swimming in different directions to symbolize the two extremes of this sign – the heights of saintliness or the depths of depravity and escapism.

Make the most of your imagination and intuition now and you won't put a foot wrong, for you're about to discover delicious hidden depths in yourself. Even if you're not normally very creative you'll view life in a highly artistic and supremely sensitive way, whether you develop talents and skills you never knew you had or just appreciate the entertaining efforts of others. Romantic reveries are also on the cards, for you'll be deluged by fervent feelings of love and affection.

Water, especially the sea, is very important to you at the moment, and being near it or in it will help you relax. Something else that means a lot is beauty, for you won't be able to abide anything or anyone that's ugly, unpleasant or upsetting.

You'll also be a sympathetic listener to folk in need of a shoulder to cry on, for you're happy to help others without thinking of what you'll get in return.

Reversed meaning

Beware the fantasy factor, for all is not as it seems at the moment. Maybe someone's trying to run rings around you or lead you up the garden path, or you're busy deluding and deceiving yourself into only believing what suits you? Either way, you should think twice before committing yourself to anything important or irrevocable and even then you must take care, for your mind could still play tricks on you.

If you're worried about anything then those anxieties could turn into psychosomatic aches or ailments, or perhaps you'll escape into a world of your own where reality doesn't exist? Go carefully now! Be warned of addictive crutches such as drink or drugs that could create long-term problems.

. . . in the First House

Proving your love and affection for someone may involve a sacrifice although you won't count the cost. You have an ethereal quality about you that will bedazzle the folk you meet. Sea greens and other aquatic shades will bring good fortune.

. . . in the Second House

There's more to life than making money, and now's the time to put your spiritual and material values into perspective. If you're desperate for cash then jobs that are refined, arty, glamorous or which help others will bring home the bacon.

. . . in the Third House

Sympathy and compassion come easily now, which is good as a close companion needs to pour their heart out to you. You may also meet someone who has a strange but serene effect on your mind, or even completely alters your way of thinking.

. . . in the Fourth House

If you want to feel more in tune with yourself then consider moving to an abode that's near water. One of the clan could need help with an emotional matter that's worrying them more than it should. You must help them to see sense.

. . . in the Fifth House

If you need some ravishing romance in your life then it's about to arrive in the shape of a super sweetheart, but don't idealize them so much you forget they're only human. A theatrical or artistic experience could also thrill you to the core.

. . . in the Sixth House

A visit to a hospital or doctor is needed either by you or someone you know. If your work involves being of service to others then it'll bring you great satisfaction now, as will any job that's glamorous or geared towards women and beauty.

. . . in the Seventh House

If you've put your partner on a pedestal then don't be surprised when they tumble off their perch. There's more than a whiff of deception in the air, but who's fooling who? If you've always put others first then start considering yourself instead.

. . . in the Eighth House

Sexual fantasies and erotic thoughts will turn you on, for you're supremely sexy and sensuous, but don't get so carried away that you lose all grip on reality. Someone will thank you for a past service in a way that's poignant but pleasing.

. . . in the Ninth House

Being near water fills you with pleasure now, but you might soon be crossing it for a very important reason that changes your whole life. Words of true love could come from overseas or maybe you're enthralled by spiritualist or religious teachings?

. . . in the Tenth House

Where's your life heading? If you don't know, then any career with an artistic or glamorous slant is right up your street, and anything associated with creating an image is also ideal. Let your ego take a back seat whilst more selfless energies rule.

. . . in the Eleventh House

A friend means so much now that you don't know if it's physical love or something more spiritual. The focus is on your future but don't seize opportunities unless they embrace your spiritual principles. A Piscean could be very influential.

. . . in the Twelfth House

You're more psychic than ever before, so use this wonderful energy whilst it lasts. A convincing sign or message will come from someone who's passed on, and which you must follow up. Don't be afraid, but tune into the higher forces around you.

38 Rat

Divinatory meaning

The Chinese sign of the Rat symbolizes someone who can be frank and forthright, but might also be a lovable rogue (the figure on the card is dressed in a very flamboyant fashion) whose clever and quick conversation can't be taken at face value.

Act the opportunist, wheel on your considerable charm and you should do very well indeed now! In fact, you'll succeed at whatever you turn your hand to, whether it's connected with business or pleasure.

You're also full of confidence in your own abilities, which is grand if you're usually a wee bit shy and retiring, for it'll help you put your name on the map. As you'll see from the illustration on the card, the Rat's very self-assured indeed!

Your popularity's on the rise too, so surround yourself with friends and family and bask in their convivial company. Children will also mean a lot, whether or not they belong to you!

Communications are also ace, for you're able to express your true feelings now and can also sweet talk your way in and out of trouble. Jump at any travel oppportunities that come along.

Reversed meaning

You're not one to beat about the bush at the moment, but take care that your candid and honest approach doesn't lead to hurt feelings, ruffled feathers or you putting your foot in it! Folk on the receiving end of your truthful tongue may not take kindly to some of your comments now. On the other hand, beware of using your gift of the gab for the wrong reasons. Even so, you're too charming and popular to lose friends that easily for they enjoy your roguish ways - and you can always talk them round again!

Something else to beware of is being so ambitious and eager to succeed that you aim too high and end up achieving nothing at all. Try to take things a wee bit slower, otherwise you could spoil your chances for the future. People may talk with forked tongues, and someone's far from genuine and just too glib for words. Be warned of a smooth operator!

. . . in the First House

You must be alert, acute and astute if you want personal plans to succeed. Outwit your rivals by keeping mum and playing your cards close to your chest. Refining your image and banishing any unattractive traits will help you to forge full steam ahead.

. . . in the Second House

Use your current canny, clever and cunning approach to cash concerns, and investigate savings schemes and other pecuniary projects that will bring you a nice nest-egg. Someone may try to take you for a financial ride. Watch out!

. . . in the Third House

You could be in the limelight, or perhaps be seen as a pillar of the community, but unless you act in everyone's best interests a secret enemy may try to do you down. A brother or sister may seem the soul of generosity, but are they telling the whole story?

. . . in the Fourth House
Your home and family will be important to you now, even though you're restless. Domestic changes are in the offing and could bring the security you seek. One of the clan may be deceitful or dangerous, and a woman may spread malicious gossip.

. . . in the Fifth House
An amour or associate is full of ulterior and manipulative motives, so be on your guard. Get creative concepts off the ground pronto or someone could steal your thunder as well as your idea. Go carefully now or you'll fall victim to a real rat.

. . . in the Sixth House
Healthwise you'll be up one minute and down the next, and could easily catch a bug that will knock you for six. Big plans are afoot at work, but don't bite off more than you can chew. A colleague or client could try to trip you up.

. . . in the Seventh House
Close relationships look good, but you need to be independent even if your other half does feel left out or unappreciated. A friend or neighbour may seem as nice as pie on the surface whilst plotting your downfall in secret. Beware!

. . . in the Eighth House
You're in for quite a sexy interlude, but an intimate relationship may leave something to be desired. Perhaps it's time to make changes? You could benefit from someone's misfortune, but avoid gloating or feeling smug. A confidence could be betrayed.

. . . in the Ninth House
International, cosmopolitan or continental concerns call, so expand your horizons! Someone from another creed, country or culture could completely captivate you. Unorthodox, unusual or unconventional people, places and pursuits also appeal.

. . . in the Tenth House
You're aiming for the top, and you'll get there whether by fair means or foul. You refuse to be thwarted by anyone, but folk may play you at your own game or even be one step ahead. Remember that those who live by the sword also die by it!

. . . in the Eleventh House
So-called pals may let you down, betray or use you at the drop of a hat now, so be careful about who you trust. It's a fine time to join a sporting or athletic club, or any group where you can work as part of a team on a joint project or activity.

. . . in the Twelfth House
You know how to dig deep into people's minds, but watch your motives or you could get a taste of your own medicine. Some nasty folk may need careful handling. You might have to deal with someone who's unstable or unbalanced. Go carefully!

39 Ox

Divinatory meaning

Like the figure in the illustration, people born under the Chinese sign of the Ox are dependable, diligent and never afraid of hard work (think of the sacred oxen of India which are valued so highly yet toil so hard). They usually enjoy following a routine because it gives them a much-needed sense of security.

Prepare for a practical, phlegmatic and prosaic period, when you'll be the soul of reliability and responsibility. Bosses, employers and clients will all sit up and take notice of you now, for they'll see how hard-working, reliable and dependable you can be. Long-awaited rewards or recognition are certainly on the way, but don't expect them just to land in your lap or appear without any effort on your part. You might even discover hidden depths or a steadfast side of yourself you never knew you had. In fact, you're the salt of the earth now!

Traditional and conservative topics and ideas will appeal and provide a strong sense of security that'll mean a lot to you. You'll revel in the close company of kith and kin and will feel happiest safely ensconced within your own four walls. Getting out into the garden, going for long country walks or communing with nature are three good ways to relax now. It may take you time to reach your goal, but the slower the better.

Reversed meaning

It's one thing to have the courage of your convictions but quite another to stick to your guns and hold your ground when even you know you're in the wrong. Try not to be so stubborn and intransigent now, and instead see the other side of the story.

Your mind isn't working as quickly or clearly as you'd like either, and it could be hard to grasp ideas or suggestions that you usually take in your stride. Woe betide anyone who hurts you or does you down now, for you'll be determined never to forgive or forget. What you must realize is that remembering all the pain in your past will only make your more miserable in the long run. Learn to let go.

. . . in the First House

Unless you're practical and realistic in all personal affairs you'll get nowhere fast, and stubbornness or obstinacy will send you straight back to square one. A sober and sensible approach, plus your business acumen, will put you ahead of the game.

. . . in the Second House

Material and monetary matters mean a lot now, and it's a grand time to increase your long-term investments or buy stocks and shares. Avoid being greedy or avaricious or you'll lose the lot! Be honest over earthly goods and all will be well.

. . . in the Third House

Your mind may be working slowly now but once you've got going there'll be no stopping you from making your mark with an idea or suggestion. Even so, you should take things one day at a time and remember slowly but surely wins the race.

. . . in the Fourth House

What a propitious period for building or buying property, for the more security in your world the better! You can create firm foundations in familial and domestic dealings, and emotionally you're in fine fettle. You'll be happiest near your nest.

. . . in the Fifth House

Start recognizing your true worth! You've plenty to offer the world, but until you have faith in yourself many of your talents will remain hidden. Your love life looks lacklustre at the moment, even though you're feeling lusty and lecherous.

. . . in the Sixth House

You're full of vitality, although your neck and throat could be vulnerable. It's a grand time to begin a project that makes the most of your dedication, diligence and hard graft. Results won't be instant, but when they do appear they'll come thick and fast!

. . . in the Seventh House

You're looking for a relationship based on loyalty and fidelity, but that may mean having a partner who's not exactly exciting. Decide what's most important to you, then you'll live happily together, and may even enjoy some sultry, sexy surprises!

. . . in the Eighth House

Pair up with a pecuniary partner and you might make a packet – but only if it's share and share alike. Investigate insurances or investments and build up a sound financial prospect for the future. Sexually, you're red hot and raring to go!

. . . in the Ninth House

Part of you is wary of taking risks but you'll throw opportunity down the drain now unless you take a chance and discover a new side of life. Be adventurous and Lady Luck will smile on you! Cosmopolitan connections will be worth a small fortune.

. . . in the Tenth House

This is one of the most ambitious times of your life, full of empire-building, power and influence. You'll reach the goals you set yourself, but first you must plod a little and plan a lot! The older you get, the more success you'll have.

. . . in the Eleventh House

Your future hopes and wishes rest upon your desire to achieve, but any rash, reckless or rushed actions will send all your plans up in smoke. A friend who's firm and faithful may not be all that exciting, but they're worth their weight in gold.

. . . in the Twelfth House

Beware of misunderstanding other people's emotions and, more importantly, neglecting your own. You must be more aware of your feelings! Tune into psychic subjects and higher vibrations, for there's more to this world than meets the eye.

40 Tiger

Divinatory meaning

Tiger tiger burning bright! The Chinese sign of the Tiger symbolizes people who are magnetic, magical and mesmerizing, but who have to tread their own path through life. In the card the Tiger looks dazzling and is surrounded by stardust.

You're injected with a huge dose of excitement, energy and stacks of charisma, making you a very magical but rather mysterious person to have around. Your currently dynamic personality will ensure you're absolutely irresistible to others, so don't be surprised if you're surrounded by plenty of doting dear ones. You're very hard to ignore now!

Brilliant brainwaves and inventive ideas are spilling out of you at the moment, so cash in on as many as you can, put them into practice and watch your reputation shoot sky high. As a result you'll be a valuable part of any team, and your warm generosity will also stand you in super stead when dealing with others.

If you usually use your clothes as camouflage then be prepared for a most fashionable and flamboyant phase, when you'll want to stand out from the crowd and turn everyone's head! You're electrifying!

Reversed meaning

Taking a back seat or playing second fiddle could be almost impossible for you now, for you long to be a leader not a follower. You also want to make a name for yourself, and will soon feel frustrated and furious when folk ignore you or won't take you seriously. Loved ones may also accuse you of being selfish and self-centred.

If you're faced with any important choices now you could hedge your bets or shilly-shally for days rather than make a definite decision. There's also a danger that you'll get bogged down in trifling details and miss the main point, though you'll be the last person to admit you're in the wrong!

. . . in the First House

Unleash your personality on others and your interests and ambitions will soar like a rocket to success. You must be outrageous, unorthodox and controversial, for the more you're noticed the greater the heights you'll aspire to – and reach!

. . . in the Second House

Unorthodox and novel ways of making your money grow will increase your income by leaps and bounds, so be as original as possible! Your fiscal fortunes are so unpredictable that the more loot you expect the less you'll get. Expect nowt and you'll gain all!

. . . in the Third House

Your brainpower is second to none, so put forward ideas and arrange meetings or interviews for you'll impress folk with your personality and unique thinking. The woes or whims of a sibling may bore you. Some news will shake up your routine.

... in the Fourth House
You want to be unfettered by family ties and hate being tied down domestically, but that may cause upheavals, disruptions and a break from kith and kin. You may revel in chaos now but will you feel the same when it's security and stability you're after?

... in the Fifth House
You're saturated in sex appeal, but need a lover who's more than just a pretty face and will help you cash in on your terrifically creative talents. Use your potential to the full and you'll enjoy overnight success in any enterprise or venture you fancy.

... in the Sixth House
Ragged nerves are a health hazard, so learn to know when you need a rest. You're very dynamic now, but unless you can work at an even pace you'll put too much strain on others. A professional position will come from an unexpected source.

... in the Seventh House
Close alliances are stirred and stimulated by the most electrifying vibrations imaginable. If you're single then stand by for an encounter that's short but sweet. Long-term associations will go through dramatic changes too.

... in the Eighth House
Someone you meet will light your fire but be a damp squib when it comes to lusty liaisons, or maybe it's you who's all talk and no action? You may have a wee windfall, but joint money matters will suffer when one of you does sommat stupid.

... in the Ninth House
Your luck and personal fortune lies in another land, so you must leave your home if you want success and excitement. Fortune favours the brave now, so banish limitations and constraints from your world and look to a glittering future.

... in the Tenth House
You'll soon set course on a career filled with adventure and excitement, but only if you go out on a limb. Any job that involves new technology or anything unusual will bring success beyond your wildest dreams, but from an unexpected direction.

... in the Eleventh House
The future's fabulous if you grab opportunities, fly in the face of convention and not follow the true, tried and tested. Fame and fortune beckon, for miracles can happen as your life is turned upside down. An unorthodox pal will help you out of a rut.

... in the Twelfth House
Your perceptions and intuition will help you sum up situations and people with unerring accuracy and could even mean influence and glory. Act with humanity and you'll be contented, but let your ego take over and you'll soon come a cropper.

41 Rabbit

Divinatory meaning

The Rabbit in the illustration on the card looks as if she is playing a game – instead of facing up to reality she'd rather invent her own little world. Folk born under the Chinese sign of the Rabbit are so sensitive and psychic that their delicate nerves and emotions are easily upset. They are supremely creative.

The harsh and hard realities of life aren't for you at the moment, for you just can't cope with anything unpleasant or upsetting. Instead, you'd rather surround yourself with the people, places and pastimes you most enjoy and let the rest of the world look after itself.

Your current sophistication, elegance and taste will attract plenty of admiring glances, for you're imbued with refinement and more than a hint of diplomacy. It's a grand time to go shopping, for not only will you automatically choose the classiest clothes but you've also got an eagle eye for a bargain! Creative and artistic pursuits will help you express your delicate and sensitive emotions. Romance is never far from your gaze.

Reversed meaning

Unless you're careful you could find yourself in the midst of rows or ructions that'll be difficult to cope with. In fact, they could leave you feeling quite ill and deeply unhappy, especially if they involve the folk you hold most dear. You might also have to deal with people who are ugly in some way, or who upset you on a very psychic and sensitive level.

New ideas or last-minute plans will also find you at a loss, because it'll be hard to take them in or grow accustomed to the changes they bring. Beware of inflicting your bad moods on others, and take care that your naive and unworldly nature doesn't lead to confusion, delusion or misunderstandings when dealing with others.

Take care of your escapist tendencies and of over-indulging in far-reaching fantasies.

. . . in the First House

The gentle touch will give you what you want from life, so the more demure, tender and soft you are the better. Adopt a kind and caring attitude and admirers will flock to your side. Cultivating and improving your image will also pay off.

. . . in the Second House

Tread carefully in all monetary matters and beware of being too trusting, gullible or naive, for canny crooks or slick salesmen could take you for a ride or part you from your cash. Try to be more sceptical and don't take everything at face value.

. . . in the Third House

The rat race is not for you now, so withdraw from rowdy, raucous or stressful surroundings and head for places that are pretty, pastoral and peaceful. You'll soon feel better! Try to take a neighbour or relative's hard luck story with a pinch of salt.

. . . in the Fourth House

Home is where your heart is, for domestic dealings look grand. If you've felt low then you're about to be revived. A celebration or reunion is on the cards, so why not stage the party at home? A lovely emotional experience is on the way.

. . . in the Fifth House

Ravishing romance is just around the corner, imbuing you with glamour and refinement, but don't idolize the object of your affection and forget they're only human. Artistic and creative concerns are ace, thanks to your imagination and talents.

. . . in the Sixth House

You've a deep desire to help those in need, and a hospital visit is possible, whether you're the patient or the visitor. Drink or drugs could have weird side-effects. Put your ego on the back burner at work, for the more selfless you are the better.

. . . in the Seventh House

You're putting your partner on a lofty pedestal, so be prepared to find they have feet of clay. You could be idealizing all your relationships now, seeing folk only as you'd like them to be. Come down to earth fast, or you'll be heading for heartache.

. . . in the Eighth House

You long for a sexy but sentimental sweetheart, but are your wishes more fantasy than fact? It could be a long time before your Prince or Princess Charming arrives, and even then they won't be perfect. You'll benefit from someone's generosity.

. . . in the Ninth House

Travel plans could easily go awry now, or what seemed a dream destination may prove very disappointing indeed. Why not read travel books or brochures instead? A wee fling with a foreigner is possible even if you do stay at home.

. . . in the Tenth House

Ambitions count for nowt, and instead you want to welcome contentment, fulfilment and peace of mind into your life. They'll mean much more than material success. If you're searching for a career then choose one with an artistic or selfless slant.

. . . in the Eleventh House

Before forging ahead on future projects you need to ensure your plans aren't just pie in the sky, for there's a danger you're being unrealistic and impractical now. Maybe you should seek the advice of a well-meaning and objective friend?

. . . in the Twelfth House

Make the most of your psychic powers now, for they've never been stronger. Read books or join societies that help you channel your intuition. Unless you can learn to tune into yourself you'll fall foul of neuroses and worries that will hold you back.

42 Dragon

Divinatory meaning

There is something very theatrical and dynamic about the exotic Chinese sign of the Dragon, as shown by the figure on the card. Just as the dragon breathes fire, so these people can be so intoxicated by their own innovative ideas that they're fired by enthusiasm into being impulsive or impatient.

Personality plus! You fairly snap, crackle and pop with vitality, vibrance and vim at the moment, so there's no chance of you being ignored or taken for granted. Instead, folk will marvel at your exuberance and energy, and you'll revel in their admiration and applause. In fact, your will-power's at an all-time high now, helping you to do anything you want and ensuring the folk around you share your strong and unbreakable belief in your own abilities. Make the most of this time and you could go very far indeed!

You're also a real perfectionist at the moment, unwilling to accept second best or to produce anything inferior yourself. Let's face it, you're larger than life now, and are filled with so much enthusiasm that anyone would think you were breathing fire!

Reversed meaning

Beware of being boastful, arrogant and too full of your own importance now, for you could easily switch from being surrounded by a theatrical and dramatic aura to being a right old prima donna! Having a strong sense of pride is fine but not if it means you bridle and get hot under the collar every time it's dented! In fact, you could have to watch your temper now, even if you're usually easy-going, calm and controlled. All sorts of silly things might make you see red, or perhaps you'll just be impulsive, irritable, impatient and only too eager to fly off the handle?

What you must watch, though, is harbouring grudges or resentments, for that will only lead to unhappiness and misery in the future. Try to forgive!

. . . in the First House

You're utterly irresistible at the moment, so if you want to impress anyone or push ahead with personal ambitions, now's the time to do it! Your electrifying charisma and personal magnetism will attract others, but only if you think and act big!

. . . in the Second House

You're living on credit far too much, and unless you've got the collateral to back up your big ideas you'll invite trouble galore to your door. But if you can finance your enterprising projects and business ventures, then there'll be no stopping you!

. . . in the Third House

Someone loves the sound of their own voice – is it you? Ensure you can come up with the goods before you make any promises, and insist on receiving your due if you're waiting for facts or figures. Take news or views with a pinch of salt.

... in the Fourth House

Prepare for fireworks at home, for you're ready to fly off the handle at the slightest provocation. You've no time for relatives who try to restrict you, and kids could goad you once too often. Check electrical wiring and beware of fire hazards.

... in the Fifth House

You're so sexy and amorous that you'll attract admirers by the score, and adore a flurry of flirting and philandering! Creatively you're second to none and are destined to succeed, so use your energy, dynamism and impetus to the full. What a star!

... in the Sixth House

You're firing on all cylinders now, so don't burn yourself out! There could be news on the work front but double check it 'cos not everyone's as honest as you. Channel your energy in the right direction and you'll make your fame and fortune!

... in the Seventh House

It's hard to relate to others now for you're only interested in yourself. It's a grand time to marry or pair up with a partner, but will you feel the same once the novelty's worn off? If you can't curb your conceit you could end up very lonely indeed.

... in the Eighth House

You're giving out some lusciously lusty and voluptuous vibes, but are you really as sexy as you seem or are you just teasing? A shared financial arrangement may look good on paper but could you make more by yourself? Beware of being selfish now.

... in the Ninth House

Adventure beckons, so fly off into the wide blue yonder! The further you go and the more enterprising you are, the more excitement you'll have. It's a grand time to protest over a misfortune or injustice, but only if your cause is honest.

... in the Tenth House

Success! That's what you crave now, and you won't do anything by halves in your efforts to achieve your ambitions. Once you've done that you'll shout your triumph from the rooftops! You've got what it takes, but can you sustain this pace?

... in the Eleventh House

The path you tread through life is of prime importance now, 'cos you're bored and browned off with things as they stand and want to hit the big time. You've tons of talent, but need the support of firm friends to steer you towards success.

... in the Twelfth House

Take it easy! You're so keen on having a good time that you're missing out on a whole host of subtle, sensitive and spiritual sensations and influences. Meditate or ponder on life's richer experiences, and happiness will be yours.

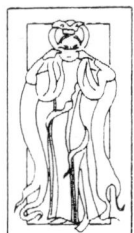

43 Snake

Divinatory meaning

One look at the illustration on this card should tell you volumes about the Chinese sign of the secretive and seductive Snake. These people are mysterious and unwilling to reveal their true motives or feelings and can seem very cold-blooded on the surface in order to mask their fervent and fevered feelings.

You're full of mystery, depth and hidden charm now that'll leave lots of folk helpless in your hands and as soft as putty when it comes to getting your own way. In fact, this is the card of the *femme fatale*, who exerts her wonderful wiles to ensure she gets the upper hand. In the illustration, the female Snake looks like Mata Hari!

Making the most of your good looks will pay delicious dividends, for you're even more attractive and sexy than usual. It's perfect if you're trying to turn a pal into a paramour, for how can they resist you? Especially in skintight clothes, snake-hips!

Money-making schemes will also fare well, for you're a financial wizard at the moment, especially if you listen to your instincts and let them take the lead.

Reversed meaning

Just like a python with its prey, you could hold on so tightly and tenaciously to loved ones now that you strangle and smother them with your love. Beware of being possessive or clinging, or you'll lose the very folk you want to keep. The odd thing is you could be very flirtatious or even unfaithful yourself, but heaven help a partner who plays you at your own game! You'll do anything to get your own back!

Although you'll find it easy to amass money at the moment, parting with the pounds will be much harder and might even make you seem miserly and mean. Try to show folk your true self, even if it goes against the grain, otherwise they'll misconstrue your motives and see you as sinister, cold and manipulative. Take care!

. . . in the First House

You're being plagued by the green-eyed monster, but instead of being eaten up by feelings you can't control, why not channel that energy into your own pet projects? Bring out your bewitching charm, make the most of your allure, and you'll be riding high!

. . . in the Second House

Money matters mean everything to you, but don't make them the be-all and end-all. You're about to receive offers you'll find hard to refuse and may stand on the threshold of riches, but don't use loot for the wrong motives or you'll lose the lot.

. . . in the Third House

You're radiating charm and excitement, but unless you're open and honest folk may misunderstand you. Instead of keeping your thoughts to yourself, discuss them with others. You'll be asked to keep a secret, but it might be kinder to spill the beans.

. . . in the Fourth House

Possessions and property increase your sense of security. It's a grand time to consider moving house or putting down your roots, but only if it's a change for the better. A member of the family will show their true possessive colours, or could it be you?

. . . in the Fifth House

Powerful passions could easily run away with you now, but don't allow amour to turn into an obsession. Why not channel all those compulsive energies into creative or artistic activities instead? You could bring out talents you never knew you had!

. . . in the Sixth House

A mysterious illness or ailment may lay you low, or you could pick up more than you want from a sexual partner. Your working world looks good, with the chance to gain power or promotion. Beware of someone who throws their weight around.

. . . in the Seventh House

There's more than a whiff of jealousy and possessiveness in the air, but is it you or your partner who's been bitten by the green-eyed monster? You must find a happy medium and sort things out otherwise you'll be in for a tearful time.

. . . in the Eighth House

The death of a situation or person will alter your whole outlook and fill you with feelings deeper than any you've known. You'll benefit from the loss or misfortune of another, and will have to face a dilemma that evokes many hidden emotions.

. . . in the Ninth House

You're attracted by the unethical and immoral, yet want to stick to your own high standards. Find a happy medium, but act for the general good or you'll soon come unstuck. Someone from another clime or culture may not be all they seem.

. . . in the Tenth House

Power's what you're after now and you're all set to get it, thanks to your superb ability to plot and plan. But keep your motives above-board, otherwise folk may play you at your own Machiavellian game. Don't let your ego get out of hand either!

. . . in the Eleventh House

Friendships are powered by mixed fortunes now. A so-called chum may be seething with suppressed envy and resentment towards you. On the other hand, you might enjoy the love and loyalty of a true pal who helps you with your future hopes.

. . . in the Twelfth House

If you're trying to make ends meet then seek help from voluntary groups or the social services. Don't be tempted to profit at the expense of anyone who'll seek revenge, for there are some very menacing forces at work. Try to adopt a more spiritual stance.

44 Horse

Divinatory meaning

Just like a horse galloping along, people born under this Chinese sign of the Horse hate feeling fettered or trapped. They need to be on the move, and also need plenty to occupy their agile brains.

Pulsating with personality, you're also imbued with stacks of sex appeal and oceans of attractiveness at the moment, ensuring your popularity's at an all-time high. Make the most of it whilst it lasts! Folk will also enjoy your super sense of humour and practical approach to life. Been thinking of throwing a party or staging a celebration? Then swing into action now whilst you're the host or hostess with the mostest!

Instead of being frightened by hard work you positively leap at it now, especially if it brings out your current competitiveness and need for knowledge. You'll be able to make important decisions in an instant, even if you usually can't make up your mind, so no wonder your prestigious and professional prospects are looking so good!

Reversed meaning

Childish outbursts and tantrums are in the offing now — are you the one who's stamping their feet in frustration? If not, then you could have to deal with someone's perfectly reasonable demands — just as long as everything goes their way, of course! In fact, they'll be deeply disgruntled and profoundly put out whenever things go against them.

Everyone makes mistakes, but the actions you're taking at the moment seem to show you haven't learnt from yours. Think before you act, otherwise you could find yourself repeating mix-ups and muddles from the past that'll leave you with egg on your face. Something else to watch is being inconsistent or even irresponsible, which will really put you in other people's bad books.

Make sure you finish anything you start: you're apt to change horses mid-stream and let yourself and others down.

. . . in the First House

You're galloping towards success, thanks to your optimism and opportunistic attitude. The more chances you take the further you'll go, so don't take a back seat when you could be a front runner and all set to win the Gold Cup of life!

. . . in the Second House

Continue with your current cavalier capers with cash and you'll soon spend the lot! Instead, seek the advice of sober and sage folk in the know and investigate investments and savings schemes. The more others help you, the better you'll fare.

. . . in the Third House

Advertize your brilliant brainwaves to influential folk and you'll do well. Be sure to voice your opinion or speak your mind, and you'll dazzle others with your articulate and erudite views. Stuck in a rut? Remember, variety is the spice of life!

. . . in the Fourth House

It's time to nurture family ties and the very roots of your world, even if you would rather be out enjoying yourself. Making loved ones feel appreciated now will ensure they'll do the same for you when you need some help.

. . . in the Fifth House

Stand by for a fabulous flirtation when the more mentally you're matched the longer it will last. Creatively, you're brimming with good ideas, but you must finish all the ventures you begin, otherwise you'll just be frittering away your time.

. . . in the Sixth House

Take steps to soothe your frayed and fretful nerves now, especially if you're feeling at your wit's end. Give yourself the chance to unwind or your health will suffer. Get some exercise, try a new diet and work out a revitalizing regime.

. . . in the Seventh House

Close relationships must be built on friendship and mutual understanding, and it's time to improve a particular partnership by talking things through and being honest with each other. Your alliance has reached a make-or-break stage!

. . . in the Eighth House

You're in a supremely sexy mood, but beware of conducting a clandestine courtship as rumours will be rife or you could be the loser in an eternal triangle. Instead of being devil-may-care in joint money matters you must stiffen your backbone!

. . . in the Ninth House

The gypsy in your soul is crying out for release, making you long to travel far and wide. Use your keen judgement to create or chase opportunities now and success will be yours. Just make sure you don't abandon projects halfway through!

. . . in the Tenth House

Is your career or vocation trying or limiting? Then it's time to change to a professional path that gives you free rein to express your ideas, intelligence and versatility, and to communicate with the world at large. You can do it if you try!

. . . in the Eleventh House

Friendship's what you need now, so how about joining a club, group or society? You're about to meet a fabulous new friend, but you'll fare best as platonic, not passionate, pals. A plan for the future looks ace, but only if you follow it through.

. . . in the Twelfth House

Your inability to express your inner emotions is about to injure intimate affairs. You must cultivate compassion, sympathy and tenderness, otherwise you could sabotage a precious partnership. Tune into life's higher vibrations!

45 Sheep

Divinatory meaning

The Chinese sign of the Sheep represents people who are cosy, caring and considerate, and who adore being in their own homes – the woman on the card is holding the key to her house, and looks as if she's about to do lots of cooking and cleaning.

Maternal, compassionate and kind – that's the way to describe you at the moment. This is the sign of the perfect home-maker, so make the most of this opportunity to gather the clan around you or turn your abode into a delicious den of comfort and pleasure. Family matters will be high on your agenda now, and you'll feel unhappy and unsettled if too many miles part you from your loved ones. You'll be happiest when you're at home.

Artistically, you shine like a true star now, whether you bring out your own talents or just enjoy the efforts of others. But enjoy yourself you will, especially if that involves fabulous food, cherished company and the chance of a good belly laugh. No wonder so many people want to be near you! You're also supremely sensitive and emotional now, and anyone needing a shoulder to cry on need look no further than yours.

Reversed meaning

You may be brimming with good intentions, a big heart and a sympathetic nature, but other people aren't. In fact, there's a strong chance that nefarious or negative folk could take advantage of you now, either running rings around you or deceiving and deluding you in a most Machiavellian manner. Take care!

Security means everything to you at the moment, but try not to cling on to the past or stick close to loved ones just because you're afraid of change. Your increased sensitivity might also make you see slights where they don't exist, or go into a deep depression at the first sign of rejection or criticism. Try to grow an extra skin!

. . . in the First House

The gentle touch is what you need to show, for the more kind and caring you are now, the better the prospects for your personal ambitions. Act aggressively, be selfish or rush at things and you'll invite opposition and resentment. Take care!

. . . in the Second House

It's time to splash out on domestic gadgets, items for the family or something with nostalgic overtones. An act of generosity, kindness or charity on your part will be repaid with dividends, even though you won't have wanted anything in return.

. . . in the Third House

Feeling downtrodden or dissatisfied? Then fight your current apathy and speak up pronto, or you'll have no one to blame but yourself when you don't get what you want. Family matters cause concern and a sibling may take advantage of your good nature.

. . . in the Fourth House

Make your home the centre of your world and you'll have all the comforts and happiness you need. A new member of the clan will fill you with pleasure. It's a terrific time for motherhood and domestic matters, so bask in the warmth of family.

. . . in the Fifth House

You're soon to meet someone who'll care for you deeply, but you could be put off by their clinging nature – unless you're the one who won't let go? News of a baby, pet or pregnancy will gladden your heart, and creatively you're on fabulous form.

. . . in the Sixth House

Workaday dealings look great, especially if your job is connected with the home, domesticity or involves meeting the public. Look after yourself on the health front otherwise you could be prone to stomach trouble or women's ailments.

. . . in the Seventh House

What a pleasurable and propitious period for partnerships! An engagement, anniversary, celebration or blast from the past will stir up super sentiments and memories. Even if you're a loner you'll find someone to love now. Enjoy yourself!

. . . in the Eighth House

You don't want lust without love, but is someone whispering sweet nothings just to get their wicked way with you? It's a romantic time, but maintain a little mystique! A shared money matter will do best if it's linked with long-term savings.

. . . in the Ninth House

Opportunities are all around you, so don't be narrow-minded or short-sighted about what's on offer or you could miss out! It's a grand chance to join an ecological or environmental campaign or crusade, and put your money where your mouth is.

. . . in the Tenth House

You may think you're not ambitious but you're really longing for success. Even so, treading on other folk's toes on your way to the top or doing everyone down will do more harm than good. Fatherhood or paternal instincts may figure in your plans.

. . . in the Eleventh House

The ball's in your court when it comes to a future plan, especially if you can take the lead and be assertive and go-ahead. Want to spice up your life? Then curry favour with the right people and you'll soon be having a high old time!

. . . in the Twelfth House

You're in the midst of a very emotional patch, making you supremely sensitive and vulnerable. Romance is high on your agenda, but don't let your heart rule your head, indulge in negative escapism or justify something you know to be wrong.

46 Monkey

Divinatory meaning

The mischievous Monkey is inventive, imaginative and innovative, and folk born under this Chinese sign are never lost for words. They can juggle with words just as the monkey on the card is juggling with fruit, and can talk themselves out of the tightest corners, even telling a few white lies if that's the only way to get themselves out of trouble.

How clever can you get! Your brain's buzzing with intelligence at the moment, making you eager to absorb as much knowledge and information as you possibly can. Cash in on your current creative and inventive mind in any way you can, and you'll be acting like the typical Monkey who never lets an opportunity pass by. If you normally can only tackle one thing at a time then you'll also be amazed at your sudden ability to juggle all sorts of activities and projects at once.

You're also ace at using logic and reasoning to sort out problems now, and if they don't work then you can fall back on your considerable charm to get what you want. You could charm the birdies right out of the trees, and you'll also be able to fast talk your way out of trouble. Feeling restless? Travelling to pastures new will soon satisfy your curiosity and roving spirit.

Reversed meaning

There's no doubt your brain's firing on all cylinders at the moment, but beware of being too clever, crafty and cunning for your own good! In fact, there's more than a hint of sharp practice or even deception in the air, and it seems only too likely that you're at the bottom of it all. Stay away from anything that smacks of underhand dealings, for even if they come up trumps now they'll backfire on you in the long run.

Something else to watch is your over-active imagination, for it could easily turn fiction into fact until you believe the huge whoppers you're telling everyone. Tread very carefully indeed now or you'll really be storing up trouble for yourself!

. . . in the First House

Bring out your dazzling personality to the full! The more creative, clever and witty you are, the more admirers you'll attract. If you're out of your depth when chatting to folk then make things up or pretend you're in the know. It can't fail!

. . . in the Second House

Cash in on quick thinking and you could make a mint! Adding another string to your bow will help fill the coffers, but beware of get-rich-quick schemes or folk on the fiddle. You'll either be too clever for your own good now or really realize your assets.

. . . in the Third House

If it's promoted and publicized in the right way, you've got an idea that could make you the star of your neighbourhood, so don't keep mum. You may hear news that completely changes your life. A close relative might need steering out of trouble.

. . . in the Fourth House

It's all go on the home front, with visitors, entertaining and perhaps an important anniversary. You may also visit some far-off relatives. A teenager may land themselves in serious trouble, and younger children could be in need of control.

. . . in the Fifth House

A brief but loving tryst is on the cards – enjoy it whilst it lasts! You're a genius when it comes to creative concerns, so broadcast your brainwaves or make the most of your mental and manual dexterity. You're about to shine on life's stage!

. . . in the Sixth House

Keep a weather eye open for ailments connected with your heart, lungs or nerves, and don't force the pace or you'll be frazzled and fraught. You'll soon have to make a decision that will totally alter your working world. Everything comes in twos now.

. . . in the Seventh House

Make an effort to communicate with partners and you'll save yourselves from sticky situations or minor misunderstandings. If your other half tells you a lie then you must decide whether it was deliberate or to save your feelings in some way.

. . . in the Eighth House

Some sexual intrigue may be on offer, but don't be surprised if it's a bit too hot to handle or acts as a real eye-opener. An agreement or transaction involving shared finances or possessions will do well but a little sharp practice may be going on.

. . . in the Ninth House

You should travel to find your fortune now, so don't rule out a move to another town, county or country. It could be the making of you! Don't believe all a politician or VIP tells you, and even a legal matter may stray from the truth.

. . . in the Tenth House

If your career or job leaves you stuck in one place, bored or unfulfilled, then you're ripe for a change. You need a profession that's busy, energetic and full of life, especially if it involves communication or travel. Off you go!

. . . in the Eleventh House

You'll soon be attracted to a group or organization that changes your life and are also about to make an important new friendship, but only if you get out and about. Keep yourself to yourself now and you won't realize your full potential.

. . . in the Twelfth House

It's time to recharge your mental batteries by investigating anything mysterious, mystical or metaphysical, and you might even become an expert tarot reader or astrologer! You may also be invited to join a secret society. Sounds intriguing!

47 Rooster

Divinatory meaning

Anyone born under the Chinese sign of the Rooster is a true individual and eager to strike out on their own. They are full of advice, whether it's been asked for or not, and can be pedantic, precise and sometimes very critical.

No-nonsense and down-to-earth, that's you at the moment. You'll do things in your own way and ignore the comments of others, for you're sure you're right. What's more, your current candour will probably make you say so! One area in which you'll truly excel now is organization, for your mind is marvellously methodical, practical and precise. Bosses, superiors and colleagues will all be impressed with your ability to arrange people and projects, so swing into action now whilst you're so capable and controlled. Even so, you could be a wee bit rebellious when the need arises!

You're also neat, tidy, analytical and decisive now, and you'll find it difficult to cope with folk who dilly-dally or can't make up their minds. You might even treat them to a few home truths if you get really exasperated!

Reversed meaning

Ouch! Voicing your opinions is second nature now, but you may not have realized just how harsh and hard they sound to the folk on the receiving end of your wit and wisdom. You must remember that no one's perfect - not even you! – and give people the benefit of the doubt sometimes instead of coming down on them like a ton of bricks. Something else to watch is taking a high moral tone, for you could easily sound like a prig or prude when hearing of other people's misdemeanours, and that might make you very unpopular indeed.

Money's also on the agenda at the moment, but you'll either spend every penny you've got or put a padlock on your purse! Watch out as well when it comes to work, for you might make promises now that you can't deliver. You're also likely to upset the apple cart by being overly critical or just plain vain.

. . . in the First House

You must be matter-of-fact now or you won't enjoy all the advantages coming your way. Distance yourself from folk or circumstances that will upset or worry you and take an analytical approach, then you'll be able to push ahead progressively.

. . . in the Second House

Money matters must be tidied up immediately if you're to work out where you stand financially. Pay any bills or final demands that have piled up, balance your books, keep a record of what you spend or apply for a loan. Come on, be cash-conscious!

. . . in the Third House

To err is human, to forgive divine. That's the motto to remember now for you're far too keen to carp and criticize others, but what makes you think you're so perfect? Stop being a bit of a know-it-all and study your own imperfections for once!

. . . in the Fourth House

No matter what the season, your home needs a massive spring clean 'cos it's currently chaotic! Emotionally you may be rather aloof, so try not to be too detached when someone needs sympathy. A woman may need help but don't try to run her life.

. . . in the Fifth House

A loving liaison's about to hit problems, but placing the blame on each other won't help one bit. Instead, why not show some warmth and tenderness to your amour? Adopting a calm and rational approach to an artistic activity will ensure its success.

. . . in the Sixth House

Want to get on at work? Then be sure of your facts and figures, be professional or start studying for extra qualifications. Odd ailments may turn you into a bit of a hypochondriac, but could the real cause be undue worry? Learn to relax!

. . . in the Seventh House

Your close relationships are all iced up, and someone's got to start a thaw. One of you may be happy with the way things stand whilst the other is longing for a change, and the only way to sort things out is to talk them through. Try a little tenderness!

. . . in the Eighth House

It's a difficult period in your deeply personal relationships as you can't reveal your emotions or even feel anything now. Work out what's wrong and then seek professional help if necessary. Joint business or commercial concerns will excel.

. . . in the Ninth House

You're torn between trying your luck away from home and fulfilling the duties expected of you. Weigh up the situation carefully, discuss it with others if necessary and trust your own judgement. An educational course or study may also interest you.

. . . in the Tenth House

Keep cool, calm and collected even if you're in a state inside, pursue your goals through knowledge and efficiency, and you'll soon achieve success and prestige. Making the most of your organizational skills will really catch the boss's eye.

. . . in the Eleventh House

A close companion will help you map out your future. It's a smashing time to delve into the pros and cons of long-term plans so you know what they involve. The more careful and controlled you are, the better your chance of success.

. . . in the Twelfth House

Much soul-searching is needed for you're faced with a situation you find hard to handle. Someone's bewildering behaviour may try your patience, but don't be too hard on them. Studying yoga or meditation will put you in touch with your feelings.

48 Dog

Divinatory meaning

Devoted, considerate and faithful, people born under the Chinese sign of the Dog have many steadfast supporters and affectionate admirers. Their ability to put others first and themselves second can turn them into drudges or doormats at times.

Man's best friend! That's the main message of this card which foretells a time of devotion, loyalty and reliability. No wonder this is said to be the most popular and likeable of the twelve Chinese signs! Whatever your usual personality, you'll put others before yourself now, especially if they've been hard done by or are less fortunate than yourself. In fact, you could act like a magnet for underdogs, lame ducks or folk who are down on their luck, and you'll be eager to right any injustices you hear of.

Beware of getting bogged down by detail now, for you could easily lose sight of what's important. One thing that will matter to you, though, is being surrounded by beautiful objects and possessions that are precious to you, for you've got a strong need now to steep yourself in the little luxuries of life.

Reversed meaning

You've got a desperate desire to be liked by everyone you meet now, but beware of letting that need for approval turn you into a victim who'll put up with anyone or anything. You might also be taken for granted by people who are only too eager to cash in on your good nature. If so, then try to say no when they ask you to do favours, and realize that you can't please everyone all the time! If you don't it could lead to trouble, for although you'll put up with a lot of rough treatment now even you will reach breaking point eventually! And then woe betide the person who's done you down! Trying to forgive and forget could be beyond you now, but be warned that bearing grudges or harbouring resentments will only make matters worse in the long run.

. . . in the First House

Be friendly and honest in your dealings with others now, even if they do irritate and annoy you. The plight of one who's an underdog will rouse you into defending their rights against uncaring folk. Your smile will break down many barriers.

. . . in the Second House

The less money means to you now, the better you'll fare financially and the more civilized your dealings will be. Mixing business with pleasure will ensure negotiations and meetings go with a swing. A profitable and productive pecuniary period!

. . . in the Third House

Convivial, congenial and chatty, you're great at putting people at their ease. Discussions, debates, interviews and get-togethers will all see you shine, especially if you have to sell yourself or an idea. Banish any laziness and strike whilst the iron's hot!

112

. . . in the Fourth House

You're playing happy families, thanks to your ability for compromise and diplomacy. Intervening in domestic disputes will avoid further trouble, whether they concern you personally or are someone else's problem. Spread a little happiness!

. . . in the Fifth House

You're a grand matchmaker for others but your high ideals make it hard to choose a swain for yourself. Remember, no one's perfect and we must all make allowances! Artistic and creative concerns look great, but can you be bothered to make the effort?

. . . in the Sixth House

Watch your diet and take some more exercise, otherwise you'll feel liverish and sluggish. If you're taking a back seat at work then expect a blasting from your boss, but if you're putting in the elbow grease your commitment will soon pay dividends.

. . . in the Seventh House

You're very loyal and loving, but are easily upset when your partner doesn't meet your high expectations. Come on, take 'em as you find 'em and stop expecting your other half to act like a saint! Otherwise, you'll both be heading for unhappiness.

. . . in the Eighth House

A hot-blooded fling is on the cards! It may not last long but it will have important repercussions in your intimate affairs and awaken complex and profound passions inside you, leading to vital realizations about how much relationships mean to you.

. . . in the Ninth House

You long to explore pastures new and may even want to emigrate. A trip abroad will either strengthen that desire or make you count your blessings at home. Use your head not your heart when making decisions. An injustice will make your blood boil.

. . . in the Tenth House

You're quietly ambitious but want to reach your goals with the minimum of trouble. However, you must realize that your path to the top will introduce you to adversaries and rivals, and only an iron hand in a velvet glove can cope with them. Be strong!

. . . in the Eleventh House

You're more popular than you could ever imagine, and may soon meet folk who'll become loyal followers, helping you personally and with plans. It's not what you know but who you know that matters now, so cash in on your contacts quick!

. . . in the Twelfth House

You seem highly emotional on the surface, but you can be quite aloof and cold when you want to be. If you're faced with a crisis now, try to tune into other people's emotions or you'll be accused of just going through the motions and not really caring.

49 Boar

Divinatory meaning

Folk born under the Chinese sign of the Boar love a simple life and are the salt of the earth. They take trials and tribulations in their stride and their patience and perseverance can set a shining example to others. However, they adore *la dolce vita* and can really overdo the food and drink, as you can see on the card.

Whatever your usual mode of life, you've got very simple tastes and needs at the moment. You're also eager to please, ensuring your popularity and making you great fun to be around. Family life's particularly important to you now for you're feeling very big-hearted, but you'll also enjoy being with fond friends and close companions, especially if it's a good excuse for a party or celebration! In fact, if there's one thing you'll enjoy at the moment it's having a good time!

Your current earthiness and steadfast ways mean you won't change tack once you've embarked on a particular path, even if it ends in disaster. Instead, you'll stick to your guns. You're also full of courage and fidelity now, and dear ones will be able to count on your love and support come what may. Endurance and patience are your watchwords now!

Reversed meaning

You'll run in the opposite direction at the first hint of clashes, conflict or confrontation now, for you just can't cope with nasty scenes, fights or rows. Try not to let things reach such a painful pass, for you could easily find yourself giving in to bullies or browbeaters simply for the sake of keeping the peace.

You're blessed with a huge and loving heart at the moment, but you'll find it hard to cope if your darling spurns your amour or lets you down. The green-eyed monster might also rear its ugly head in the form of overpowering jealousy. If you're on a diet then prepare to fall by the wayside, for you could easily overdo *la dolce vita* in a very exaggerated and excessive way. Cheers! Gross self-indulgence and debauchery are indicated; you just don't know when to stop!

. . . in the First House

Enjoy life to the full, forget your worries and indulge yourself in the luxury, leisure and pleasure of life! If you've been acting a wee bit high and mighty or putting on airs and graces then come down to earth a little – it'll endear you to others.

. . . in the Second House

Acquisitions and possessions are very important now, for you need to ensure you're financially secure. Look into ways of making money, supplementing your income and investing for the future, but watch your motives. Beware of being too extravagant.

. . . in the Third House

You believe in calling a spade a spade, but you need to know when to be frank and forthright and when to be a wee bit more tactful. It's good to be honest, but don't be so blunt that you go too far and put people's backs up. Be subtle sometimes!

. . . in the Fourth House

Someone's treating kith and kin like possessions rather than people, so make sure you're not the culprit. A woman is especially obstinate and obdurate now, but being stubborn in return will only make her more inflexible.

. . . in the Fifth House

Sexy and sensuous describes you now, but beware of letting amours think you love 'em when really it's only lust. Artistically you're on top form, so enhance and channel your creativity by making full use of your smashing potential.

. . . in the Sixth House

You may adore the good life but too much will take its toll, so try to combine good living with plenty of exercise. If you want what money can buy you must be prepared to work for it, so don't slacken the professional pace!

. . . in the Seventh House

Want to make your relationship truly happy? Then one of you must learn the art of true romance. There's no disputing the superb fidelity between you, but showing each other how much you care will ensure your amour goes from strength to strength.

. . . in the Eighth House

Lusty, lascivious and very, very sexy, you're about to embark on an affair that's pure animal, but is it what you really want? A productive pecuniary partnership will be forged now, and if you're awaiting payment or alimony you'll get your fair share.

. . . in the Ninth House

Enjoy the green green grass of home and forget about travelling at the moment. Opportunities will arise on your own doorstep, so don't wander too far afield or you'll miss them! Don't be jealous of someone else's lot for you're in clover now.

. . . in the Tenth House

A slow, steady and certain stairway to success is ahead of you, and patience, determination and commitment will pay off. You long for enough loot to buy all the luxuries you long for, so stay in control and you'll soon be sitting pretty.

. . . in the Eleventh House

A faithful friend will loom large in your long-term plans now. Trust in their judgement and help for they really do have your best interests at heart. Join a society associated with nature, agriculture or music and you'll make a valuable new pal.

. . . in the Twelfth House

Seeing is believing for you, but it's time to investigate the psychic and mystical mysteries of life, delve deep into your inner emotions and get in touch with the higher forces around you. If you're low on loot then ask about benefits and grants.

50 Mercury

Divinatory meaning

Mercury was the winged messenger of the Roman gods (he was known to the Greeks as Hermes), and was given his winged cap and the wings on his feet by Jupiter, the king of heaven. In astrology, the planet Mercury is connected with communications and rules the two signs of Gemini and Virgo, which both excel at communicating.

Communications are the key to success now, so grab every opportunity to put your feelings into words, express your ideas and make contact with folk who live near or far away. It's a super time to write letters, make phone calls or arrange meetings, especially if they're connected with buying and selling. If you feel restless or bored with your usual surroundings then day trips or short jaunts to nearby places will be exciting and interesting. Cars, bikes and other modes of transport could be important too.

Try to meet, mix and mingle with folk who are on your light-hearted but intelligent wavelength. You've no time for bores or bigots now! You'll enjoy the company of kids and will have fun playing card games, doing crosswords, reading books or anything other pastime that makes the most of your brain cells. It's an especially favourable card for Geminis and Virgos.

Reversed meaning

Watch out, there's mischief about when Mercury's reversed! Communications could easily go awry, with phones on the blink, letters going astray, messages muddled or folk getting the wrong end of the stick. Try to delay any important meetings for the moment, especially if you've got to sign on the dotted line or conclude a deal, for you may not have all the facts to hand.

Children could play up or maybe you meet someone who's mischievous or mendacious? There might also be problems connected with neighbours, close relatives or your local environment. Take care of downright lies and petty pilfering.

. . . in the First House

Your powers of expression are vital to your personal success, so promote yourself, put forward your ideas and get in touch with folk who will further your cause. Writing, reading and talking will put you at the top of life's league!

. . . in the Second House

Cash in on your superb skills at buying and selling, add the right amount of publicity, and you'll double your money! Don't take anyone for a financial ride or the boot will be on the other foot one day. Writing could help pay the bills.

. . . in the Third House

Use your brilliant brain and you'll be like a soul inspired. Arrange interviews and meetings whilst you're so silver-tongued and eloquent, and bluff your way through any subjects you don't understand. It's a very busy time and a short trip's needed.

. . . in the Fourth House

Moving house? If not, you should consider it for you'll find more luck and happiness in another abode. If you must stay put then some home improvements will do just as well. A visit from a relative is on the cards and you'll be travelling yourself soon.

. . . in the Fifth House

Amour is about to put zest and zeal back into your heart and it's just what you need! A child will also play an important part in your world now. Bring out your creativity, especially if it involves writing, for it could lead to stunning success!

. . . in the Sixth House

Your frayed nerves suggest you should slow down, stop pushing yourself so hard and not take on so many things at once. If a visit to a hospital or doctor is needed then don't delay any longer. Your working world's ready for a change-round.

. . . in the Seventh House

Communications are imperative in close relationships, for unless you can talk about your problems or worries you'll drift apart. If everything's grand already then do more together. Two heads are better than one in business matters.

. . . in the Eighth House

Secrets surround you now, but if you're asked to keep a confidence then mind you do, for blabbing will backfire on you. Discuss any sexual problems with your other half and sort through outstanding insurance or pension matters.

. . . in the Ninth House

Don't wait for an excuse to go travelling – your itchy feet are just longing for the off! Any international links forged now will be very fruitful indeed, and you'll be thrilled and fascinated by another country's cultures and customs.

. . . in the Tenth House

If your career's becoming a bore then maybe it's time to find fresh ways of using your initiative. Ideally you'd like to follow two paths but can you give them equal attention? Jobs that combine communications with travel or teaching will be ace.

. . . in the Eleventh House

Carefully thinking through a long-term plan or project could mean you're on to a winner, as one flash of genius is all you need for success. A turn in events could alter your future in the twinkling of an eye, perhaps thanks to a Gemini or Virgoan.

. . . in the Twelfth House

Mystery and suspense grip your mind, so why not write a spine-chilling story or start studying astrology? A psychic experience will only increase your interest. You'll have to sort out a secret soon before it becomes public knowledge.

51 Venus

Divinatory meaning

Known as Aphrodite to the Greeks, Venus was the Roman goddess of beauty and love who sprang from the waves after the mutilated body of Uranus had been thrown there by Saturn. In astrology, the planet Venus is associated with femininity, love and beauty, and is the ruler of the two Sun signs of Taurus and Libra which are both associated with these charming characteristics.

As the illustration on this card suggests, love and affection are all around you now, but don't forget they come in many forms. You might meet the man or maiden of your dreams who really sweeps you off your feet, ensuring that life will never be the same again! If you've already paired up with a partner then your loving liaison will go from strength to strength, thanks to the spirit of give and take flowing between you. In fact, being with all your loved ones will warm your heart. Compromise and conciliation are also in the air, so swallow your pride, kiss and make up if you've clashed with a close companion.

You might also fall for an artistic enterprise, or any other activity that gladdens your heart and fills you with satisfaction. Beautiful people, places or possessions also mean lot. Taureans and Librans will fare especially well now.

Reversed meaning

You may be full of love and fond feelings for the folk around you, but take care for your motives may be misconstrued. Maybe someone mistakes your affection for amour, or you come on so strong that you seem manipulative or self-centred? Arguments may be anathema to you at the moment, but don't be so keen on a quiet life that you let others walk all over you or shoulder the blame for something you didn't do.

Spending money will be highly enjoyable, but don't get carried away or you could end up broke, or fork out on luxuries that look good in the shop but seem gaudy when you get them home. Watch your weight, for your willpower's at an all-time low! Be warned of an avaricious or envious woman.

. . . in the First House

You've got to change your image and make the most of your looks if you're going to make progress, so get out the mirror and give yourself the once-over. The more ardent and loving you are now the better. Say it with flowers or a kiss!

. . . in the Second House

Prosperity is assured and wealth yours for the taking! Your fortune lies in any money-making activity associated with love, women or beauty. Instead of being envious of others' possessions, remember it's what money can't buy that matters.

. . . in the Third House

Entertaining others will be of benefit to you, whether in business or pleasure, and folk will adore your charm and winning ways. Be seen in the right places and success will be yours. News from a close female relative will gladden your heart too.

. . . in the Fourth House

Happiness at home is predicted, for your kith and kin hold all the answers now. Buying something lavish and luxurious for the abode will add to the harmonious atmosphere. A female relative will proclaim her love or announce her wedding.

. . . in the Fifth House

Love in its most wonderful and radiant forms is about to come your way! A super someone may sweep you off your feet and alter your life entirely. It's time to capture your heart's desire, for whatever or whoever brings you pleasure is within reach!

. . . in the Sixth House

Take care of your throat, back or kidneys as they're vulnerable now. Your working world is very happy at the moment, giving you the chance to go places, so don't hold yourself back by being idle or indolent. You must be prepared for hard graft!

. . . in the Seventh House

Happiness is ensured in all your close relationships, and whether you're embarking on a love match or a professional partnership it will be prosperous and highly pleasurable! Caring and sharing bring rich rewards, so settle any arguments now.

. . . in the Eighth House

You're exuding oodles of sexual excitement, and using your erotic charms will get you anything you want. A past kindness of yours could be repaid with a windfall, and all joint financial agreements are destined for wealth and wonderful gains.

. . . in the Ninth House

Love and travel are linked now. Perhaps water will separate you from an amour, you'll live with your sweetheart away from your native land or you'll fall for someone from abroad? Cosmopolitan contacts will bring riches and love into your life.

. . . in the Tenth House

Success awaits you in professional matters if you make the most of your looks, ready to catch the eye of a boss or VIP. You could make money from the way in which you deal with the public. Your charm will get you anywhere at the moment.

. . . in the Eleventh House

A woman or female friend is your guide, mentor and supporter, and words of wisdom will show you the right direction for the future. Apply for financial backing for long-term plans now. A link with a Libran or Taurean will be grand.

. . . in the Twelfth House

Take care, for you could begin a romantic relationship that has no future, or fall victim to unrequited love for one who's far out of reach. A secret affair may be exciting but beware of double-dealing or deception from a so-called amour.

52 Earth

Divinatory meaning

This card shows Atlas, a descendant of Jupiter, holding up the world. Atlas was a king who owned many beautiful and fruitful gardens, but he was condemned by Jupiter to support the world on his shoulders. In astrology all the planets of the Solar System are considered to revolve around the Earth, so no Sun signs are ruled by it.

You're in a practical, matter-of-fact frame of mind now and able to view life from a sane and sensible viewpoint. In fact, you've got your feet firmly on the ground, making you a good person to have around in a crisis! You'll be keen on sticking to the status quo, but don't let that make you afraid of trying something new or striding out in different directions when the need arises.

Environmental or ecological causes and campaigns could appeal to you now, especially if you're looking for a new interest in life, because you'll enjoy doing your bit to save the planet. Nearer to home, working in your own garden or on an allotment will also be productive, especially if you can grow your own food.

Reversed meaning

You're a real salt of the earth figure at the moment, but don't get so carried away with being a stoic that you try to carry the weight of the whole world on your shoulders! Folk who are down on their luck could easily take advantage of your good nature now if you let them, so stand up for yourself if you're turning into an agony aunt or uncle.

Another possible problem is being a bit of a stick-in-the-mud, or very narrow-minded in the face of progress. Don't cling to the past or old-fashioned beliefs just because you're frightened of facing up to the future or taking a chance. Closing your mind to fresh possibilities could mean you miss out on a lot of opportunities and openings. You've a tendency to turn a blind eye to the serious harm being done to Mother Earth, and may even be contributing to it.

. . . in the First House

A pragmatic and practical approach is the path to success now, so adopt a more down-to-earth attitude if you're usually a bit airy-fairy. Interesting yourself in the environment, ecology or conservation will be rewarding and very valuable too.

. . . in the Second House

It's a fine time to increase your income and strengthen your material security through savings schemes or investments, but don't set so much store by possessions that you lose sight of the more valuable spiritual and emotional prizes life has to offer.

. . . in the Third House

It's the simple things of life that bring you pleasure now, from community concerns to chatting with neighbours. You may be asked to help conserve or improve part of your neighbourhood. Make any overdue phone calls or polish off outstanding paperwork pronto.

. . . in the Fourth House

Wallow in the comfort and peace of your home sweet home, especially if your domestic world has been shaken or stirred lately, and those emotional wounds will soon start to heal. Take life slowly, commune with nature and just relax. Bliss!

. . . in the Fifth House

Passion is coursing through your veins, so grab your sweetheart in a close clinch! All alone? Well, you may not stay single for long! A baby or pet may make you feel loved and needed. A creative venture could bring lots of loot your way.

. . . in the Sixth House

The stresses and strains of everyday life may take their toll, or maybe you fall victim to colds or headaches? Herbal or homoeopathic remedies will help, but having a rest is the best cure of all. Jobs connected with natural products fare best now.

. . . in the Seventh House

Loyalty, fidelity and old-fashioned values are accentuated, making permissive or impermanent partnerships fall by the wayside. Instead, if your relationship is founded on total adoration and complete commitment you'll be in clover!

. . . in the Eighth House

You're sizzling with a strong sexuality that'll make you very hot stuff, so let's hope your other half's in the mood for love! It's also a grand time to embark on joint financial projects with a passionate or pecuniary partner.

. . . in the Ninth House

You like the idea of travel and adventure but are loathe to leave the safety of your home! How about visiting family or friends overseas so you've got the best of both worlds? Working on green issues will benefit both you and Mother Earth.

. . . in the Tenth House

The simpler your ambitions, the better chance they have of succeeding now. Financial recognition and promotion are on the cards if you work with money, the land or property, as long as your intentions are honourable and you don't get greedy.

. . . in the Eleventh House

Joining a group, organization or society whose soul purpose is to preserve and protect the planet could have magnificent results, and your sterling example may soon have friends following your lead. In fact, all humanitarian causes will do well now.

. . . in the Twelfth House

Folklore, myths and legends intrigue and thrill you, and you'll discover mediumistic or intuitive talents that will enhance your life. Discover more about the supernatural and occult, for the world's a most mysterious and mystical place.

53 New Moon

Divinatory meaning

In astrology, the New Moon is believed to represent the beginning of life. At the time of the New Moon astrologers encourage people to make new beginnings, fresh starts and renewed efforts. A New Moon occurs when the Sun and Moon occupy the same sign of the zodiac.

This is a marvellous opportunity to embark on new projects, seize the initiative and put your ideas into action. If you've got any plans or projects on the drawing board, this is your chance to get things moving. It's also a smashing time to embark on a new venture or chapter of your life, such as joining forces with like-minded folk, signing contracts or starting another job. A house move or new home is strongly indicated.

You're also imbued with extra energy, vim and vigour now, giving you a head start when it comes to competing with others and filling you with the drive and dynamism needed to get cracking on the schemes and dreams that are close to your heart. Don't waste a second in making the most of this fortuitous card! Be prepared for a baby's birth.

Reversed meaning

Dragging your feet, holding fire or procrastinating are all likely now, for you seem unable to exert any effort or enthusiasm. New opportunities might await you but somehow you just can't work up the energy to do anything about them and it seems you'd rather let them slide. Getting to the bottom of your current lethargy and laziness could provide the cure, so think hard about what's wrong. Maybe you're frightened of chancing your arm on something new, and letting yourself down in the process, so you'd rather do nowt? Clinging on to the past instead of marching boldly into the future could be another problem, but you must learn to look ahead with confidence now.

. . . in the First House

You're standing on the threshold of some wonderful new beginnings when you'll be able to explore and discover a host of exciting experiences. Be prepared to take the initiative and you'll be on your way to personal happiness, success and fulfilment.

. . . in the Second House

A prosperous and fruitful phase beckons, when you can increase your income, add to your savings and build up a nice nest-egg for the future. All you must do is grab opportunities as they arise, for you'll miss out all round if you take a back seat now.

. . . in the Third House

Your current environment's as stale as can be, but you may not know it. Be logical and think things through, and you'll soon see you need a more stimulating and satisfying life. Go out on a limb if needs be, cock a snook at your critics and get a move on!

. . . in the Fourth House

A domestic cycle's coming to a close, so reorganize your current abode or move on to pastures new. Put yourself in a position that will safeguard your security, increase your sense of belonging and blot out the pain of your past. A new life is calling!

. . . in the Fifth House

Whether you produce a baby, an idea or a creative masterpiece, it's time to grasp the nettle and use your innate gifts to the full. A new loving liaison's also on the cards, when you'll meet a super sweetheart or fall for your darling all over again.

. . . in the Sixth House

Make a fresh start in your working world, for you're being offered the chance to begin again, whatever your current circumstances. Renewed vitality will also help you overcome any ill health, ensuring you're fitter than you've been for years.

. . . in the Seventh House

Engagements, weddings or anniversaries are on the cards as all partnerships enter a purple patch of happiness, harmony and tenderness. It's a wonderful chance to repair rifts and rebuild relationships or embark on a chapter of rapture with someone new.

. . . in the Eighth House

You'll soon meet someone who'll make you sizzle sexually! Grand if you're single but what if you're not? If fidelity means a lot to you then why not spice up your current love life instead of jeopardizing it for what could be very deep emotional waters?

. . . in the Ninth House

Your destiny could lie in far-off lands, giving you the perfect incentive to make a brand-new start. If you're staying put then expand your horizons by studying or adding to your qualifications. A brave new world is opening up now!

. . . in the Tenth House

Glittering prizes await you down the path of fame and fortune, but first you must seize the initiative and grab every professional or prestigious opportunity going. Be prepared for a change in direction or even a new career. Anything goes now!

. . . in the Eleventh House

The merit and dignity you possess will help you enjoy a firm, fruitful and fulfilling future. Long-term hopes, wishes and dreams must be put into action if you want them to succeed. You'll also meet someone who will help you map out your future.

. . . in the Twelfth House

Don't be surprised if you're swept off your feet by a stunning sweetheart! Tuning in to your psychic powers will give you a good guideline to follow, and folk will adore the aura of serenity and kindness that is shining around you.

54 Full Moon

Divinatory meaning

The Full Moon signifies the end of life in astrology, but on a more general level the time of the Full Moon indicates a good opportunity to tie up loose ends and bring matters to a tidy conclusion. A Full Moon occurs when the Moon and Sun are in opposite signs of the zodiac.

An episode is about to come to a close in your world, but look on it as an opportunity to clear away the dead wood in your life ready for the marvellous new experiences to come. Clinging on to the past or dwelling in days gone by is a mug's game now, so grit your teeth, view your life with honesty and clarity, and eradicate everything that's no longer valid, viable or vital. It will be poignant, and even painful, at the time, but the actions you take now will really pay off in the months and years to come. In fact, once you've taken the bull by the horns you'll probably feel relieved, refreshed and wonder why you didn't do it earlier! Remember, as one door shuts so another one opens, and you're about to discover the truth of that for yourself. Your home and emotional security take on added significance.

Reversed meaning

It's still a time of change, but you may have little control over what happens now. Enforced alterations or irrevocable partings could tear at the very fabric of your life, especially if you're unprepared for them, and you may feel powerless in the path of destiny. Allowing yourself time to grieve over the past and come to terms with what's happened will be invaluable when you're ready to build a new life for yourself. A profound belief that out of bad comes good will also pay off. The area of the spread in which this card falls will tell you more about its effects, especially when you examine the other cards around it. There could be bereavement and loss, or just a temporary parting of the ways, but expect tears and sadness whatever happens.

. . . in the First House

A chapter in your life is drawing to a close, signifying a highly sensitive and emotional time when you must turn your back on any parts of your world that have outlived their usefulness, and look to the future instead. Why not update your image as well?

. . . in the Second House

Money matters are getting out of hand, so make amends before the rot really sets in. Get a grip on your extravagant streak, begin to budget, seek advice if needs be and revise and refine your pecuniary policy until at last you live within your means.

. . . in the Third House

It's no good clinging on to the status quo any longer for the cards are telling you to climb out of your current ruts and routines and completely alter your everyday existence. Some news on the way will really bring home to you it's time for a change.

. . . in the Fourth House

Changes to home and family life are inevitable now if you're to achieve the emotional happiness and contentment you deserve. Maybe you must sever the apron strings at last, stop dwelling in the past or say farewell to a loved one, but do it you must.

. . . in the Fifth House

Put selfish motives to one side now and act for the good of others instead. If there are problems with a loved one then you must put him or her first and yourself second, and the same goes for any creative enterprises you're involved in.

. . . in the Sixth House

Alterations to your work or daily doings are essential now, so don't fight the changes that arise because you'll benefit in the long run. Get to the root of any depression or worries, otherwise they'll spark off all sorts of odd ailments.

. . . in the Seventh House

If a liaison is over then try not to cling on when you know you should really let go. Someone will soon fill the gap! On the other hand, maybe you need to reach a new understanding with a partner, so your relationship can continue to grow and mature.

. . . in the Eighth House

Face up to hang-ups, inhibitions or emotional complexities now, whether they come from you or your other half, for they must be dealt with once and for all. Abandon an affair if it's founded on false feelings, ready for something more satisfying.

. . . in the Ninth House

The finger of fate is pointing overseas, for that's where your future lies. You're soon to make a long journey or meet someone from foreign climes who'll show you what the world's got to offer. Cutting your old ties will be painful but productive.

. . . in the Tenth House

If you're a round peg in a square hole or unappreciated then you must move on to a career or position that will bring out your true talents at last. You'll be too busy and happy for any regrets! Success, honour and self-esteem await your decision.

. . . in the Eleventh House

Whether you know it or not, you need to rethink or reconsider your hopes and wishes for they're no longer relevant. A true pal may not be around for much longer, but they'll pave the way for an even greater and more meaningful friendship.

. . . in the Twelfth House

Getting to know the inner you is imperative for your health, happiness and spiritual contentment, so start delving deep into your subconscious, even if that does mean facing up to some unpalatable parts of your personality. You'll benefit in the end.

55 Mars

Divinatory meaning

The ancient Romans believed Mars to be the god of war, while the Greeks called him Ares. Mars had many amorous adventures, including an embarrassing episode with Venus, so in astrology, the planet Mars is linked with masculinity and strong sexuality, and thus rules Aries and Scorpio which are also associated with these characteristics.

Stand by for a surge of energy, enthusiasm and enterprise, when you'll be raring to go in every area of your world. You're eager to make a name for yourself at the moment, thanks to an ego that won't take kindly to being ignored or given a back seat. You want to be a leader, not a follower, so put your best foot forward and show folk you mean business! Amorous affairs find you hot-blooded, and erotic – just what you need to revive a flagging love affair or stagnant sex life! Sporting and athletic activities also appeal and help you burn off any excess energy that could otherwise turn into aggression or arguments.

Speaking your mind, or being blunt and to the point, is important to you now, but take care you don't go overboard and hurt people's feelings! Arians and Scorpios will thrive now.

Reversed meaning

Batten down the hatches, for there's more than a whiff of bad temper and tantrums in the air. You could fly off the handle, bite people's heads off or snap at them for no reason at all – or so they think. What you must do is work out why you're acting like a bear with a sore head, and then do something about it.

If sticky circumstances have got you feeling frustrated and furious then channel all that ire and irritation into physical action. Gardening, walking, sports or DIY will all make you feel better. Your libido's also on the rise now, but don't be too selfish sexually or make your partner think you're only after their body.

Mind how you go when using sharp knives or hot objects, for you could be very accident-prone.

. . . in the First House

Be assertive, dynamic and quick off the mark and you'll get what you want from life, so grab the opportunities that come along and jettison anything about your character or image that could hold you back. There's no stopping you now!

. . . in the Second House

Money-making propositions are just around the corner, so leap at the ones most likely to succeed. He who hesitates is lost, so act the aggressor, pull your weight and force the issue. If at first you don't succeed, then try, try again. You'll do it!

. . . in the Third House

Start treading whichever path gets you out of your rut and into the fast lane of life. Be prepared to make instant decisions, move like lightning and seize the initiative, otherwise you may miss the chance to alter your everyday existence for the better.

. . . in the Fourth House
A man in the family circle is making life difficult at the moment, but are you the reason he's so moody and insecure? If so, then patch things up pronto! Check all domestic gadgets and appliances that could be a fire risk.

. . . in the Fifth House
Cupid's arrows are flying left, right and centre, making it a very lustful, lecherous and lascivious time indeed. How hot-blooded can you get! Take the initiative and don't delay in a creative enterprise, and keep an eye on a naughty child.

. . . in the Sixth House
A change in your working world is in the offing, but only if you're bold, brash, brave and make the first move. Even though you're busy you must look after your health, especially if you're having headaches. You're also accident-prone.

. . . in the Seventh House
Relationships are nowt to write home about now thanks to someone's selfish and arrogant actions, but unless you can compromise, conciliate and acquiesce where necessary, things will go from bad to worse. Stop saying 'I' and start saying 'We'.

. . . in the Eighth House
Get set for a stunningly sexy time, whether you're swept off your feet by someone new or rekindle the fires of passion with your other half. Whatever happens, love and hate will be closely connected. A joint cash concern could cause contention.

. . . in the Ninth House
Be frank, fearless and forthright otherwise you'll end up with nothing now. Making a decision will involve taking a risk, so live dangerously and opt for adventure, and excitement! An Australian or Canadian contact will fill you with enthusiasm.

. . . in the Tenth House
You're raring to go, but concentrate on fulfilling just one burning ambition or you'll fritter away all your energies. A prestigious or professional opportunity is on the way, but let your new-found power go to your head and you'll fall from grace.

. . . in the Eleventh House
The idea a man plants in your head now will help you to fulfil many of your hopes and dreams, but only if you strike whilst the iron's hot, make the first move and act the entrepreneur. Join a sports club and you'll meet a marvellous new mate.

. . . in the Twelfth House
Jealousy, resentment and revenge rear their ugly heads now, so study close relationships carefully. Steer clear of anyone who's compulsive or coercive, and sever any clandestine connections before they blow up in your face. You have been warned!

56 Jupiter

Divinatory meaning

Jupiter (known as Zeus to the Greeks) was the most powerful of the ancient gods and ruled the kingdom of heaven. In astrology the planet Jupiter is linked with expansion, plenty and luck – in the card Jupiter is holding a cornucopia of four-leaved clovers. The planet rules the Sun signs of Sagittarius and Pisces.

This a grand card to appear in any spread, for it represents abundance, benevolence and good fortune aplenty. Anything from lucky breaks to once-in-a-lifetime opportunities will arise now, especially where making money is concerned, so leap at every opening and advantage that comes your way! Acting the entrepreneur, being optimistic and having a positive approach to life will bring rich rewards, for you'll attract pleasant, productive and propitious people and events to your side. It's also a time of laughter, enjoyment and revelry, so dip into the treasure trove of good times and bonhomie that Jupiter's offering you! Sagittarians and Pisceans will be especially lucky.

Expansion is also the order of the day, so broaden the boundaries of your brain through intellectual, philosophical, metaphysical or cosmopolitan concerns. Travel, higher education or global enterprises are all favoured too.

Reversed meaning

Steady on! Jupiter is still a fabulously fortunate card even when reversed, but it's warning that you could go overboard in a big way now. Maybe you'll bite off more than you can chew in a job or project, over-estimate your own abilities or find you're way out of your depth in an important discussion or dealing? You might also make promises you can't keep. If your social life's swinging, then beware of over-indulging in rich food and drink, otherwise your waistline or liver could suffer. You might also end up broke! Another possible problem is being so full of your own abilities that you become boastful or too big for your boots. Try not to blow your own trumpet quite so loudly, and remember no one's indispensable – not even you! You're only human after all, despite what you think.

. . . in the First House

Opportunity knocks! You're about to enjoy enormous personal growth, but don't bite off more than you can chew or all your great expectations will come to naught. Even so, you can afford to take a few risks, thanks to your guardian angel!

. . . in the Second House

Money, possessions and status symbols make your eyes light up now, but beware of extravagances unless you can afford them. Yes? Then speculate to accumulate and watch your assets grow. Business and property deals look especially good.

. . . in the Third House

Ease yourself out of life's ruts, expand your world and think big! Educating yourself or using your brain more will give you the edge over others. Any communications connected with cash will bear fruit. The luck of a close relative could rub off on you.

. . . in the Fourth House

Buying a new abode? If not, then how about it, or perhaps you'd rather spend money improving your current home? It's also a grand time to treat yourself to a few luxuries or labour-saving devices. One of the clan could strike it rich now.

. . . in the Fifth House

Amour's all around you, so welcome it into your world. Leisure and pleasure will bring you lots of happiness, and Dame Fortune's on your side in both loot and love. A gift that represents your heart's desire is on its way, fulfilling your dearest wish.

. . . in the Sixth House

Prosperity and productivity march hand in hand in business plans, so act with positive initiative in all workaday dealings. Just make sure you can deliver the goods before you make any rash promises! Feeling below par? Treat yourself to a tonic!

. . . in the Seventh House

One-to-one affairs glow with happiness and laughter, making it a terrific time to pair up with a partner. Business dealings are also ace, though you'll fare best if you're part of a team. A former enemy may come over to your side.

. . . in the Eighth House

Your luck and destiny are currently controlled by a close companion, making you rely on their support. Delve deep into pensions, insurances and investments and conclude any financial agreements. A legal or tax matter needs prompt action.

. . . in the Ninth House

Your fortune lies in travel and foreign places, so fly away if you can! A foreign caller could capture your imagination too. A political, business or legal matter will go well, so force the issue if needs be but don't wear yourself out.

. . . in the Tenth House

Success is assured if you take your chances now, but don't act in a pompous or puffed-up fashion, or shoot your arrows so high they miss their target by miles. Only make promises you know you can keep and don't exaggerate your virtues or abilities.

. . . in the Eleventh House

Your future success lies away from your native land, so perhaps it's time to increase the scope of your long-term plans? Anything done in moderation now will succeed. Someone you meet, maybe a Sagittarian or Piscean, will become a good pal.

. . . in the Twelfth House

You're full of goodness and kindness, enabling you to help others as well as yourself. You'll gain in many ways by holding out the hand of compassion, but don't forget there are some folk you just can't help. Money from a secret source will be of benefit.

Divinatory meaning

Saturn was a Roman god who was forbidden to bring up any male children, although his sons Jupiter, Neptune and Pluto survived. He is shown as an old man to signify wisdom through experience, one of the characteristics associated with the Sun sign Capricorn that is ruled by the planet Saturn (also illustrated on the card). Saturn rules Aquarius too.

You could be in for a rather restricting, sober or stringent time but it'll pay dividends in the long run. Part of Saturn's message is about learning from experience, and that's just what you must do now. If you've recently made mistakes or been left with egg on your face, then think about what went wrong and how you can avoid doing the same thing in the future. Even so, you shouldn't be hard on yourself, but instead must boost your self-confidence by concentrating on all your plus points. Folk may have a much higher opinion of you than you imagine!

Your current reliability and responsibility should impress bosses and authority figures, and you could also win respect and acclaim in all professional or prestigious projects. Dealings with older folk, parents and superiors will go well too. Capricorns and Aquarians will benefit most of all from this card.

Reversed meaning

Someone's being very cantankerous, crabby and critical at the moment. Is it you? If so, then stop being so negative, narrow-minded and nit-picking, and try to look on the bright side instead. Your self-confidence could also take a big bashing, but dwelling on all your past mistakes or taking the blame for other folk's failings will only make matters worse, or plunge you into a deep depression that you'll find hard to shake off. Money may also be in short supply, forcing you to go without in some way.

Trouble with your teeth, bones or skin may also make you blue, but beware of turning into a hypochondriac and thinking you've got every ailment under the sun! It's a time when you feel deeply alone, isolated and unappreciated.

. . . in the First House

Stop underestimating your own abilities and being frightened of failure, and instead find ways of boosting your confidence and being kinder to yourself. Once you start to believe in yourself, success and happiness will surely follow.

. . . in the Second House

Money matters are in dire straits 'cos you're in sore need of loot. Maybe you're paying for others' wasteful ways or more money goes out than comes in? Well, it's time to tighten your belt, budget wisely and only spend on what you can afford.

. . . in the Third House

You're wallowing in misery at the moment, unable to communicate with others, feeling sorry for yourself and with a chip on your shoulder. The trouble is, folk will give as good as they get, so try to be less negative and instead be more sympathetic.

. . . in the Fourth House

What a mass of insecurities and uncertainties! You even think your own family's against you, but could your current problems stem from doubts and guilts instilled in you as a child? It's time to lay these ghosts from the past once and for all.

. . . in the Fifth House

Amorous affairs are going through a testing and trying time, and your own sense of inadequacy will only make matters worse. On the other hand, any alliance that spans the generation gap will do well. An adopted or fostered child may figure in your life.

. . . in the Sixth House

Take care! Your health is rather vulnerable now, so wrap up well, eat properly and head for the doctor if you're puzzled by odd ailments, aches or pains. At work you may be at the mercy of an authoritarian employer who can only carp and criticize.

. . . in the Seventh House

Tread carefully in one-to-one affairs and patch up any quarrels or strengthen any weak spots before they start to threaten your relationships. The older your spouse or the longer you've been together, the fewer problems there'll be.

. . . in the Eighth House

A crisis in your intimate affairs is stopping you having a satisfactory sex life, but perhaps you're also feeling guilty or worried about expressing your true desires? On the financial front, you must pay attention to tax affairs or pensions.

. . . in the Ninth House

You're so short-sighted, narrow-minded and blinkered at the moment! Instead of remaining in your rigid rut you must break the bonds that bind you, be adventurous and discover what life's all about. Open your mind and let experience in.

. . . in the Tenth House

Reaching the top is so important to you it could become an obsession, but try to discover what's really behind your need. If your current career's going nowhere then maybe you should choose something more suitable? Then everything will slot into place.

. . . in the Eleventh House

You'll rise or fall now according to the merits of your long-term plans, and if you've shirked or cut corners you'll be found out. Make commitment and conscientiousness your watchwords and all will be well. The advice of an old pal will be valuable.

. . . in the Twelfth House

It's time to stop worrying about everything and being frightened of your own shadow, for indulging in neuroses and paranoia will only undermine your happiness and confidence. Instead, learn to like yourself and realize your true potential.

58 Uranus

Divinatory meaning

Uranus was the most ancient Roman god of all. He was the son of Earth (Terra), but then had an incestuous relationship with her and she gave birth to the Titans, one of whom was Saturn. He mutilated Uranus, then flung his body into the sea – and Venus, goddess of beauty, rose from his corpse. In astrology, the planet Uranus is associated with change and disruption (shown on the card by all the different types of weather), and the sign it rules, Aquarius, is linked with space-age matters, originality and the occult.

Expect the unexpected! You certainly won't be disappointed, for there are changes galore on the way. They won't always be what you imagine, either, so stand by for bolts from the blue and all sorts of shocks and last-minute surprises. Maybe a partner will act out of character, you'll change your mind about something at the eleventh hour or strange situations or circumstances will take you completely by surprise? One thing's for sure – you'll be kept on your toes! Try to be as adaptable as possible, because that's the way to get the most out of this topsy-turvy time. Aquarians will be even more innovative and original than usual now. If you're restricted in any way, you will demand more freedom and independence.

Reversed meaning

Talk about intransigence and inflexibility! Someone's digging in their heels and being as stubborn as the most dogmatic donkey, and it seems nothing you can say or do will make them change their minds. Or are you the one who's gritting your teeth, holding your ground and refusing to budge an inch?

You may also have to deal with someone who seems to be flying in the face of reason, or being cranky, contradictory and downright disruptive just for the sake of it. Try not to lose your temper, for that'll only make matters worse, and ride out this eccentric storm in a calm and controlled way.

Upheaval and chaos reign at this time of your life.

. . . in the First House

You're radical, revolutionary and reforming at the moment, eager to alter everything and everyone around you whether it's necessary or not. You must follow your own star but don't be surprised if you encounter opposition along the way.

. . . in the Second House

'Completely unpredictable' is the only way to describe your affluent affairs, for you could come into a fortune or lose the lot. Better stash away some cash ready for a rainy day, just in case, for you don't know when it will arrive!

. . . in the Third House

Stand by for some significant news that will send shock waves reverberating through your world, even though you'll enjoy the chaos that ensues. You need to be noticed now, and may act in contrary or controversial ways just to attract attention.

. . . in the Fourth House

It's hard for you to settle down at the moment, especially if you're feeling trapped by stagnant, suffocating or small-minded people or places. Grab every chance to prove you're a unique individual with a mind and will of your own!

. . . in the Fifth House

You're eager for an affair or assignation with no strings attached, for you can't abide being tied down now. Creatively, you're a genius, so be as inventive as possible but resist the temptation to abandon projects halfway through.

. . . in the Sixth House

Slow down and keep calm, otherwise you'll make yourself ill. Folk in authority or who tell you what to do really make you see red and set you wondering about changing your job, but beware of leaping out of the frying pan into the fire!

. . . in the Seventh House

It's time for a radical reassessment of your romantic relationship, for divorce or separation could be on the cards. Unless you're both already free spirits then you need to inject more freedom and independence into your affair, fast!

. . . in the Eighth House

You're burning with strange sexual desires for someone you wouldn't usually look at twice, or maybe you're turned off by the prosaic predictability of your current love life? Financial gains could come from a most unlikely or unexpected source.

. . . in the Ninth House

Breaking free from your daily round is of paramount importance now, for you feel trapped by tedium and are on the look-out for excitement. You may also be drawn into a campaign or crusade, and the more extreme it is the better you'll like it!

. . . in the Tenth House

You're searching for a new direction in life, so choose one that will bring your ingenuity and independence to the fore. Even so, don't be surprised if you find success lies in unexpected quarters or comes from an unforeseen source.

. . . in the Eleventh House

Your powers of magnetic attraction have never been stronger, making you a devastating force at any social setting. You need to come up with some stimulating plans for your future, and working in a group or listening to a pal could help.

. . . in the Twelfth House

Make the most of your current intuition and powerful perception and you'll be spot on. Occult, magical or New Age subjects may make a profound impression on you. Don't fall prey to your current highly charged and complex emotions.

59 Neptune

Divinatory meaning

The Greeks called him Poseidon, while the Romans called the god of the sea Neptune. He also controlled the rivers and fountains, and could raise islands from the bottom of the sea with one blow of his trident. In astrology the planet rules Pisces, the sign of the Fish, and takes the nebulous, confused and spiritual characteristics of that sign.

Being near the sea will have an important effect on you now, and all that water will be especially calming and beneficial if you've been feeling het up or run down lately. Glamorous, sophisticated or refined people, places, possessions and pastimes also appeal, for you'll find it hard to cope with anything ugly or unpleasant. In fact, this is a terrific time to bring out your most creative and artistic talents and make the most of your imagination, for it's truly inspired now.

Ravishing and rhapsodic romance could enter your life too, either in the shape of a real Prince or Princess Charming who knocks you off your pins, or by reviving your fond feelings for your present partner. Your intuition is also on the rise, so pay attention to your dreams, hunches or insights. Pisceans are especially affected by this card.

Reversed meaning

Trying to get to the truth or picking your way through a mire of muddles and misunderstandings will be hard going now, for nothing is quite as it seems. You could be viewing the world through rose-coloured specs, or perhaps someone's trying to pull the wool over your eyes? Loving liaisons will also suffer, with unrequited love, unrealistic expectations or phoney fantasies all on the agenda. You might also discover that a paramour's passion owes more to your purse than your personality. So-called friends could reveal their true selves too, but will you notice? Whatever you do, try not to deceive, demoralize or disparage people yourself 'cos that will only store up trouble for the future. Treachery and duplicity are a dead certainty at this time.

. . . in the First House

You're more psychic, glamorous and refined than ever before, and are bound to make a smashing impression on all the folk you meet. Use your currently seductive, sophisticated and alluring quality to progress with your personal goals and interests.

. . . in the Second House

Want to make money? Then invest in the arts or antiques, or turn out your cupboards – you could unearth a treasure! You should also reassess your values and realize the best things in life are free. Spiritual matters mean more than material ones.

. . . in the Third House

Charitable acts will be repaid in kind now, for if you do a neighbour a favour they'll return the compliment. News, a letter or phone call may hold a mystery or secret that'll be revealed at a later date. A scandal or rumour may affect your reputation.

. . . in the Fourth House

Being near water will help you a lot now so how about installing a pond if you don't already live near some H_2O? A letter, keepsake or photograph will bring back memories, but see it as a symbol that you must move ahead and let go of the past.

. . . in the Fifth House

You're about to be whisked off into the arms of amour, and you'll love every minute of it, but beware of fooling yourself about something sentimental or playing games with someone's heart. A child may be running rings around you, so take care!

. . . in the Sixth House

A mystery ailment or psychosomatic problem may leave you under the weather, but what's caused it? Are you trying to avoid an unpleasant reality? Work is full of treachery and confusion, or you could be faced with redundancy or retirement.

. . . in the Seventh House

Partnerships are floating on a super sea of romance, and the more you can express your fond feelings the better. A party or anniversary could be on the cards. Watch out for someone who's out to butter you up, and view all folk as they really are now.

. . . in the Eighth House

Suggestive and seductive – that sums up your sex life at the moment. You'll be heading for disappointment if your affair is just based on physical pleasure, for love must play a part too. Only share your finances through selflessness, not duty.

. . . in the Ninth House

Investigate an ecological, environmental or metaphysical concern, or delve deep into a creed or faith that offers you all the spiritual succour you've ever wanted. Just make sure you keep your feet on the ground!

. . . in the Tenth House

Pushing your ego to the background and acting in a charitable or altruistic manner is the way to succeed now, for being selfish, Machiavellian and mendacious will get you nowhere fast. Careers that are glamorous or artistic will do well.

. . . in the Eleventh House

You'll gain a lot through actions of an unselfish and high-minded friend, so don't do them the disservice of questioning their motives. Long-term plans will fare best if they've got a humanitarian slant or you can work as part of a team.

. . . in the Twelfth House

This is one of the most mystical, magical and psychic times of your life, so why not start to develop your clairvoyant powers with the help of some expert guidance? Romance is also in the air, but only fate will decree its outcome.

60 *Pluto*

Divinatory meaning

God of the underworld, Pluto wore a helmet and cloak that made him invisible. All the goddesses refused to marry him because his realm was so gloomy, so when he fell in love with Proserpina (Persephone) he dragged her away by force. The planet of Pluto rules Scorpio, a sign renowned for its willpower and love of mystery, and also for its strong sexual urges. Revelations abound with this enigmatic planet.

Prepare for a profound and perplexing time, for the area of your world that's affected by this card will never be the same again. Pluto is the planet of complex and complete change, so get ready for a total transformation in your life. Instead of clinging on to the past or abiding by old patterns of behaviour, you must eliminate everything that's out-dated or which has outlived its usefulness. You're being offered the chance to make those changes of your own accord, but if you stand in the way of progress then matters will be taken out of your hands and you'll have to face the cataclysmic consequences.

You might also be involved in something that's secretive, mysterious or hush-hush, but you'll revel in a little cloak- and-dagger intrigue! Scorpios will be in their element now.

Reversed meaning

You need to tread carefully, for there are some very strange, intense and destructive influences around. Someone may be playing psychological games with you, using emotional blackmail to get their own way or acting in an outrageously obsessive manner. People's motives will leave a lot to be desired, and that goes for you too, especially if you let your highly-charged emotions tempt you into jealous outbursts or envious tirades. An idea, plan or project may also turn into an obsession, for compulsive or psychotic behaviour is rife.

If you've already tried to resist inevitable alterations that are transforming part of your life, then you'll find it very hard to cope with them now. Surrender to something stronger than yourself!

. . . in the First House

It's time for a total transformation of your image, identity and way of life, 'cos what worked for you in the past is no longer productive or positive. Block the path of the winds of change at your peril for they're a strong force for good.

. . . in the Second House

Financially, you'll rise or fall now according to your monetary moves. Trying to increase your coffers through sharp practice or deceit will ensure you get your come-uppance, but if you work hard and make good pecuniary plans you'll be quids in.

. . . in the Third House

You must deal with people in power now, but don't be surprised if they're drunk with their own importance or real pains in the neck! Be above-board and honest when dealing with them, and get promises or guarantees in writing, just in case.

. . . in the Fourth House

Prepare for a tear-jerking and traumatic time, when you must bid goodbye to a familiar face or place that belongs to the very roots of your world. Tread carefully when dealing with others for you could stir up bitter feelings of jealousy or revenge.

. . . in the Fifth House

Take a deep breath for you're about to plunge into very profound and intense amorous waters indeed. Keep an eye on a child's difficult and complex behaviour. Any venture or enterprise based on your talents and skills is set for success.

. . . in the Sixth House

If you're plagued by strange symptoms that are difficult to diagnose then maybe the problem stems from deep-seated worries that need attention? At work, someone may try to assert their ego at your expense or wage psychological warfare against you.

. . . in the Seventh House

One-to-one affairs are imbued with intense emotions, but beware of a partner who wants to possess you lock, stock and barrel. Dame Destiny may introduce you to someone new, but it'll be a powerful partnership that's hard to forget.

. . . in the Eighth House

Powerful passions pulsate from every pore now! You'll either entice others with your ardent aura or be dazzled by desire for someone you meet, but don't underestimate these intense emotions. You may gain through a legacy or insurance.

. . . in the Ninth House

Psychic, psychological and spiritual subjects enthrall you now and could raise your awareness and consciousness by leaps and bounds, but don't let this interest become an obsession. A cosmopolitan connection could alter your world completely.

. . . in the Tenth House

Power! That's what you want, but the danger is you may stop at nothing to get your own way – and destroy yourself in the process. Don't get involved in battles for power or issue threats unless you want to invite violence and chaos into your world.

. . . in the Eleventh House

Your long-term plans are undergoing a subtle metamorphosis, influenced by your current actions. Destiny is about to take a firm grip on your life, perhaps linking your future with that of a friend, or taking matters out of your control?

. . . in the Twelfth House

Prepare for an emotionally turbulent and masochistic time, when you get deeply involved with someone even though all they give you are tears and torment. You must end the affair, bury the past and rise like a phoenix from the ashes of despair.

61 Ascendant

Divinatory meaning

In astrology, the Ascendant is the sign that was on the horizon at the time of your birth, and describes the personality you show to the outside world – illustrated by the masks of tragedy and comedy shown on the card. (It is the right way up when the smiling mask of comedy is at the top of the card.) The sign which the Sun occupied when you were born describes your inner self and it can be very different from your Ascendant.

As the illustration shows, it is the face you present to the world that's important now, so make the most of yourself! Improving your appearance, whether it's really necessary or merely gilding the lily, will make all the difference to your confidence and give you just the boost you need to make a big splash. Treating yourself to some smart new clothes or revising your image will help attract attention to yourself, and so will turning on the charm and cashing in on your charisma. Your image is your success.

In fact, no matter how talented you are, proper presentation should be the name of your game now for everyone will take you at face value. The more witty, lively, attractive and outgoing you are, the more impressed folk will be. Remember that if you're off for a job interview or are going on a date with someone special.

Reversed meaning

Even if your world has collapsed around your ears you won't be allowed to let it show now, but will have to wear a mask of merriment instead. In fact, all appearances are deceptive at the moment, so beware of taking folk on face value or confusing a pretty appearance with a pleasant personality, for you might have a nasty surprise in store.

Of course, you could be the one who's hiding a nefarious or negative nature behind a smashing smile or pretending to be a picture of innocence when you're really as cunning as can be. If so, then watch your step for you will soon be treated to a dose of your own medicine, and you won't like the taste at all!

Your true identity is not being presented as well as it should due to your dowdy persona.

. . . in the First House

Your personality's your passport to success now, for making the most of your natural assets will propel you along the path to prosperity and prominence. In fact, you'll progress beyond your wildest expectations until you're streets ahead of your rivals.

. . . in the Second House

Using your glittering personality to the full will attract money like a magnet, for folk will be falling over themselves to help you fill the coffers. It's a terrific time for making investments, especially with the help of people in the know.

. . . in the Third House

The combined forces of your current optimism, wit, flair and style will charm the birds off the trees and influential folk into your orbit, so don't keep yourself to yourself! Meetings, negotiations and debates will all see you shine.

. . . in the Fourth House

Get ready for a cosy, comfy time when home is where your heart is and you feel safe, satisfied and secure. Your nearest and dearest will rely on you and you'll be happy to help, especially if a family celebration is in the offing. Enjoy yourself!

. . . in the Fifth House

Stay as sweet as you are and all loving liaisons will fill you with joy. There's no need to put on airs and graces for your dear ones adore you as you are. You're also personality plus, enabling you to give a creative concern just the start it needs.

. . . in the Sixth House

Even if you've felt low lately you're bursting with renewed health and vigour now. The way you project your personality is all-important in workaday dealings, so make the most of yourself and you'll earn the respect of everyone around you.

. . . in the Seventh House

Close relationships are about to blossom with joy, affection and warmth. Whether you're spoken for or not, amour will soon play a lullaby of love on your heart-strings. Teamwork is your key to success now, so join forces with a likely lad or lass.

. . . in the Eighth House

An aura of abundant sex appeal will knock everyone for six, so if you've been trying to attract the attentions of someone special this is your chance to do it! Even if you're half of a Darby and Joan duo you can rekindle the flames of passion now.

. . . in the Ninth House

Be yourself, and you'll open marvellous doors of opportunity now. You might even meet folk from other countries, creeds or cultures who'll ignite your interest in international affairs. A long journey will change your outlook on life.

. . . in the Tenth House

You're heading straight for the top, and all your aims and ambitions will be achieved. Finding a career or prestigious plan that suits your character will bring success your way, for the more you make of your stunning personality the further you'll go.

. . . in the Eleventh House

You're blessed with so much charisma and magnetism that your future's fantastic! An out-of-the-blue opportunity will offer you the chance of a lifetime that will alter your long-term plans for good, and friends will also help put your name on the map.

. . . in the Twelfth House

Inner serenity, tranquillity and peacefulness are just three of the qualities that make you so attractive to others. You're also full of compassion and kindliness, and it's this psychic energy that'll help you emotionally if you've been through a bad time.

Divinatory meaning

When they are working on a birth chart, astrologers calculate a person's Midheaven (which is the point directly overhead at the time of birth) to see in which direction their aspirations and hopes lie. The sign of the Midheaven (shown here by Icarus in flight towards his chosen goal in life) and its relationship with the rest of the chart can tell the astrologer volumes about that person's attitude towards a career, and whether it will succeed or not.

Reach for the stars! That's the message of this card, for it's foretelling that a great future's in store for you. Marvellous opportunities are on their way, particularly where your prestige and profession are concerned, so make sure you're ready to cash in on them. It's a super time to apply for a new job, put in for promotion or remind bosses and superiors of just how talented you are, for your skills, talents and attributes should speak for themselves and open many doors now.

If you've been thinking of changing your career then swing into action whilst the forecast is so favourable, and you'll soon put yourself on the primrose path to prominence and productivity. What's more, if you've been working away at a long-term project or ambition then this is when you'll see it reach a fabulous fruition. Congratulations!

Reversed meaning

Trying to make a name for yourself could be a thankless task now. Maybe you're passed by for promotion, job prospects look lacklustre or you seem to be the butt of your boss's bad temper? If so, then bide your time and don't falter from your usual high standards, for your day will come!

On the other hand, if you're resting on your laurels, getting other people to do your dirty work or think you're so clever you don't have to make an effort, then prepare for a few shocks and surprises! You could be knocked off your lofty perch, someone might show you up or you may face anything from demotion to the sack. You have been warned! After all, Icarus came unstuck, and so will you unless you pace yourself.

. . . in the First House

Your personal ambitions and direction in life should take precedence over all else now, so be single-minded and don't dilly-dally instead of striding straight towards success. Great things are within your grasp if you push forward with dignity.

. . . in the Second House

Material matters are of over-riding importance at the moment, so concentrate on swelling your coffers. Contact financial folk who can give you sound affluent advice, and make your money work for you through investments.

. . . in the Third House

Act the shrinking violet or hide your light under a bushel now and you'll really miss the boat. Set ideas in motion, arrange appointments or meetings and don't feel afraid of contacting folk who are higher up the ladder than you. You must be go-ahead!

. . . in the Fourth House

You're the master or mistress of your own destiny at the moment, and you can't afford to let tenacious family ties or a possessive relative stand in the way of success. It's time to be independent and live your own life, so sever those apron strings at last.

. . . in the Fifth House

It's all very well being a creative genius but you'll remain undiscovered unless you advertise your talents now. Sell yourself to the highest bidder, start a new enterprise or venture and get cracking. The same goes for amour – it's no time to be timid!

. . . in the Sixth House

Take the bull by the horns in your workaday world and you'll soon be riding high. Apply for new jobs, demonstrate your commercial skills and seize the initiative. Aim for what you want, both in work and health, and you'll go far indeed.

. . . in the Seventh House

If your partner's as weak as dishwater then you'll want nowt to do with them now, for you're only interested in folk as ambitious as yourself. Anyone who lets you down will be dropped like a hot brick, but the ideal relationship will head for success.

. . . in the Eighth House

You'll push ahead with any joint venture now, especially if you're expecting support or financial help. If you're looking for a business partner, then choose one who'll let you be the boss, for your current need for power won't accept second place.

. . . in the Ninth House

Your destiny is connected with cosmopolitan concerns now, so get your mind into global gear. Joining forces with a foreigner, travelling or even emigrating is your passport to prosperity. Studying and gaining more qualifications is also ace.

. . . in the Tenth House

A cherished ambition is finally coming to fruition, and the only possible obstacles are your own ego or ambition. Always be kind to folk on the way up or they'll get you on the way down. Remember that, and you'll get anywhere you want on merit now.

. . . in the Eleventh House

Formulate your plans for the future, 'cos there's no point in dreaming of success unless you know exactly how to get it. Research your facts, gather information or call on a friend for encouragement or contacts, and your ambitions will be fulfilled.

. . . in the Twelfth House

Emotional contentment and peace of mind are your goals, and they're within your grasp. If you've been gripped by irrational worries then at last you can come to terms with them and find the serenity and spirituality you've craved for so long.

63 Node

Divinatory meaning

In astrology, the Node of the Moon is a calculated point in a birth chart that reveals the karmic lessons that person must learn through life. The North Node is known as the Dragon's Head, and the South Node as the Dragon's Tail, which is why the illustration on the card shows a creature with a coiled tail which he will never be able to reach no matter how hard he tries.

The universal law of cause and effect has a special significance for you now, for this is the card of karma. Its message is simple - as you sow, so shall you reap — but its effects can be much more complicated than that. However, you'll soon taste the fruits of success, for all your hard work, selfless actions and considerate thoughts are about to receive a rich reward. It also indicates the life lessons you have come to learn from others, and what you have come to teach them, with an answer to the age-old question 'Why are we here?' — to serve and learn from our fellow men.

It's your good nature and altruism that have made you behave the way you do, and not any thought of payment in kind, but even so it's nice to be appreciated! Perhaps loved ones will show how much you mean to them, superiors will repay all your efforts or a dream you've cherished for a long time will finally see the light of day? Whether material, emotional or spiritual, you deserve all the good things that are about to arrive! (This position of the card is linked to the North Node, indicating what you give to others.)

Reversed meaning

If you've been using other people for your own ends, acting selfishly or spitefully, or doing anything else that puts you in a position of power over others, then this is when you'll get your come-uppance. Believing that material matters are the be-all and end-all of life will also trip you up now, for life is about to teach you some very hard lessons. Maybe you'll be on the receiving end of your own brand of bad behaviour or be embarrassed when the truth comes to light, but whatever happens you won't like it one bit. Why not see the errors of your ways first? It will save a lot of heartache. The reversed position is connected to the South Node, so it is here that you are learning a life lesson — this deals with what you take from others.

. . . in the First House

You control your own destiny now, because whatever you do to others you will receive in return, whether for good or ill. Proceed with extreme care, for all your actions will contribute towards your future and even trivia will have huge consequences.

. . . in the Second House

Let loot rule your life and you'll surely come a cropper now, for material decisions taken without a spiritual conscience will swiftly spell disaster and the loss of all you value. If that happens, your life's lesson will be wanting what you can't have.

. . . in the Third House

Don't put yourself above others, because acting selfishly or not lending a helping hand will leave you without a friend when you need one. The better you communicate now the finer your future, so promote and publicize your exceptional talents.

. . . in the Fourth House

There are many lessons to be learned linked with your family life and emotions, for the more love and support you give out the more you'll receive in return. You're about to face a testing time over a woman in your life, so don't let her down.

. . . in the Fifth House

Your love life is soon to present you with a karmic test, and if you put yourself first and your beloved second you'll be doomed to failure. A child or baby will have a mystical effect on you, and help you progress along the path to self-discovery.

. . . in the Sixth House

If you've been abusing your health and neglecting your spiritual welfare then it's time to give your body the respect it deserves. You must change your diet, way of life and overall outlook before circumstances overtake you and force your hand.

. . . in the Seventh House

The state of your one-to-one affairs is being determined by your own attitudes and personality, for partners will reflect your own virtues or vices. If you're always negative then you can expect a dose of your own medicine in all your relationships.

. . . in the Eighth House

Prepare for some strange sexual encounters, when your partner will either make you uplifted or unhappy. If you're inhibited about sex then you may be reliving a bad experience that could be banished by your other half's tender touch.

. . . in the Ninth House

Someone from another creed or culture holds the key to your destiny now, but it'll be a very sorry story indeed if you're prejudiced or bigoted for you'll soon meet your match. Open up your heart and mind and you'll find peace and fulfilment.

. . . in the Tenth House

Let your ego or ambition over-ride your better self and you'll never attain your goals in life. Power and success must be achieved in the right way, otherwise it could elude you forever or leave you at the mercy of a tyrannical man. Be warned!

. . . in the Eleventh House

Whatever you do now must be for the good of mankind, as only then will you gain the support and reassurance you need to succeed. Selfish aims and ambitions will be thwarted, for the lesson you must learn is to do things for the greater good.

. . . in the Twelfth House

It's a time of great psychic and spiritual awakening, when you'll be at your most sensitive and vulnerable. You're easy prey for self-inflicted worries and fears, but if you withstand such tests then happiness is yours. The answer lies within you.